Facing PTSD

A Combat Veteran Learns to Live with the Disorder

By

Tom Smith

"There's something in my head but it's not me."

Pink Floyd

Aerial Approach Inc.
PO Box 64
Keene Valley, NY 12943

—

To those who bear the battle after the war

ACKNOWLEDGEMENTS

Thanks to my early readers for your input, encouragement, and for working with such raw material:
Van Santvoord, Craig Fielding, Chris Griffin, Greg Johnson, Annemarie Reardon, Scott Swartzwelder, and Kathy Smith

And my reader-editors: Barbara Kaufman, Brad Hurlburt, Tracy McClelland, Judy Smith and particularly Arthur Westing

Special thanks to Chase Twichell for years of direction and support

INDEX

INTRUSIVE THOUGHTS

Kathy was standing at the kitchen counter chopping something on the cutting board in front of her. She looked good. A day in the sun had left a warm glow on her bare shoulders. We'd spent the afternoon at Big Beach, a wide gleaming stretch of white sand with an unobstructed view of the half-moon island of Molokini. Not the best place for waves because of the sharp shore break, but a nice place to lie in the sun.

I was sitting at the table behind her finishing a bottle of beer. We were discussing why it appeared that the longer we lived on Maui the less we went to the beach. We'd been on the island more than a year and that, I maintained, was the problem.

Kathy and I met six years earlier in a gravel pit northeast of Fairbanks. She was working for the US Forest Service, and I was flying the helicopter they chartered. From there we moved around Alaska from one field camp to another, never staying in the same place for more than a few months, often only weeks.

When we weren't working we were on vacation, traveling as far as the other side of the world. Our environment was always changing, new and interesting.

"You remember what it was like when we got here. Boogie boarding at Baldwin, hiking the crater, exploring the island," I recalled. "How much of that do we do now? The longer we stay somewhere, the less we enjoy it. I mean… that's why we left Alaska, right? We were tired of that too."

"You more than me," Kathy pointed out. "But, yeah, I was ready for a change."

I went back to watching the last of the evening light through the open porch doors. The clouds above the West Maui Mountains were bright red. Something else came to mind, and I turned my attention to Kathy.

She had finished what she was doing and was laying the large knife on the counter beside her. Before I could say what was on my mind, I saw the knife she'd just put down appear dreamlike above her exposed back and a hand, my hand, brought it down.

Stunned, I sat staring. I had just seen myself stab my wife in the back. What the hell, I wondered in awe, I wasn't even angry. The only emotion I was aware of was a growing sense of apprehension.

Was I losing it? No, I reasoned, I didn't feel weird; everything around me seemed normal. I closed my eyes and broke contact with her back. Maybe it wasn't even me holding the knife, I told myself as rationally as I could. But I saw it, felt it. It was my hand. The violent image faded quickly, but not the impression it made on me.

That moment was important. If I'd seen it another way, seen that image as random and nothing to be concerned about, the role of Post Traumatic Stress Disorder in my life may have been significantly altered. But I saw the visualization as a murderous threat to Kathy, possibly a sign of insanity, and began asking questions.

The obvious place to begin was; why would I want to stab my wife in the back? We'd been best friends since we stepped outside a bar on the Chena River and swapped life stories. The few times I'd been upset with her were the result of a misunderstanding or the consequence of a foul mood. In fact, Kathy was the most compatible person I'd ever lived with. Which, along with her unerring sense of fairness and intrinsic honesty, was the reason I felt safe in marrying her.

It didn't take long to figure out the violent image I'd seen had nothing to do with Kathy personally, so I took a look at myself, explored the possibility that it was the product of something deeper, an underlying resentment of some sort.

But what was there to resent... leaving the solitary lifestyle of a transient helicopter pilot for settling down on an island in the Pacific with an attractive young woman? Besides, I could always go back to flying in Alaska if I wanted too. Kathy wouldn't mind. She enjoyed living out of a tent in the middle of nowhere more than I did.

—

Even the old standby, "I feel tied down," didn't get any traction. The reality was, at nearly forty, putting a little distance between me and the life I'd been living the last twenty years seemed like a good idea. I had been treating my body like crap and it was beginning to take a toll.

In fact, if anyone was being tied down or trapped it was Kathy. Our age difference alone put her in the victim position. As she pointed out not long after we met, she was nine when I was in Vietnam. The more I thought about it, the more I realized that, if anyone felt resentment, it should be she.

Kathy graduated from high school when she was sixteen, paid her brother 600 dollars for his well used Chevy Impala, and left her home in Lake Forest, Illinois for Missoula and the University of Montana. Instead of going home for summer break, she took a job with the Forest Service in Alaska, a place she had fallen in love with at age ten while vacationing with her family.

After graduating from Missoula, she sold the Impala for a used 4x4 pickup truck and headed back to Alaska. Kathy was twenty-one and well on her way to see as much of the undeveloped world as she could, beginning with the forty-ninth state.

She told me about all the places she wanted to go, things she wanted to do, and for six years we did our best, traveling all over. However, since we'd moved to Maui Kathy's plans had been on hold. If I felt bad about anything, it was for not helping her see more of the world, as I had at her age. Everything considered I was glad she didn't hold it against me.

Kathy was a good woman. As far as I could tell, there was nothing wrong with our relationship, and absolutely no reason for me to want to hurt her. Once I had eliminated my wife and our marriage as factors in the bizarre, decidedly homicidal imagery, I moved on to the next consideration, my military service. In the course of a year in combat I'd killed quite a few people.

Most of the time, I didn't feel one way or the other about what I'd done. Shooting another soldier was a response to a threat, a conditioned reflex, which I did as quickly as possible. Seeing him die in front of me was the breakpoint in the fight. I rarely had time to look at it as the end of his life too. As far as feeling guilty later… I felt no less guilt for killing a man in combat than he likely did for trying to kill me. If I met his mom and dad, that might be a different story.

Without much effort I could recall gruesome images of men horribly deformed by the tools of combat, hideous representations of creatures at the end of their lives. But, they were dead. Any connection they had with me, or reality, disappeared when they died. I had very little trouble leaving them in Vietnam.

Although what I did in combat didn't bother me, I knew I brought home some baggage. Like a lot of other guys, my tolerance for noise had changed. It was as if we belonged to a club, the group that dove for cover at the sound of anything like a gunshot or explosion.

Loud music didn't bother me but a door slamming shut, anything sudden, upset me. Babies crying or someone yelling irritated me to the point of distraction if it went on very long. Also, for quite a while I slept with a loaded shotgun within reach. Not because I was frightened of anything in particular, I just felt more comfortable.

I knew those reactions weren't normal by most standards, but I didn't think they were out of place for someone who'd been a human target for a year. Regardless of what I felt or didn't feel, overall I believed that Vietnam wasn't anything more than a part of my past. However, a week or two later, while I was still kicking around the potential relationship between shooting people in a war and stabbing my wife in the back, it happened again.

As before, I felt as much as saw an extension of myself pick up a knife, and knew my intentions were murderous. Similarly it was the sight of a large kitchen knife that brought it on, but Kathy wasn't there.

Until then I'd reasonably assumed that the violent image was a consequence of her being next to the knife; that some perverse association had occurred when I caught them in a glance. But the second time she wasn't even in the room. For that matter, I realized, the knife didn't have to be there either.

The second time was also more complex. There were multiple images, feelings and thoughts, and I was a participant. Instead of observing I became involved, tried to understand what was happening, which was impossible. That's when I went from wondering why it was happening, to worrying about what was going to happen next.

5

Variations of the theme, Kathy and knives, kept cropping up. There wasn't anything I could do about the intrusive thoughts and images. It seemed that the harder I tried to curb them the stronger they became, repeatedly showing me vivid things I didn't want to see. After a couple of weeks I knew I had to tell Kathy what was going on.

One evening while she was making dinner, I asked, "Kat, would you mind putting the kitchen knives away? You know, when you're done with them." She looked at me. "In the drawer when you're finished," I added lamely as her expression went from curious to confused.

"Any particular reason?" she asked, turning back to what she'd been doing.

"Well," I began. "I've been having some weird thoughts lately."

It was a bit awkward at first, but as I spoke I felt my thoughts take shape and gain strength. The dark things lurking in my mind moved further into the shadows.

After I told her the details, Kathy asked, "So what is it? You don't like my cooking?"

"Your cooking's fine," I assured her with an appreciative laugh.

"There must be some reason you'd want to stick a knife in me?"

"It's not about you, or an urge to kill, or anything like that. It's just a goddamned thought that pops into my brain. Literally. But I can't stop it, so I thought I'd better tell you about it."

"I appreciate that," Kathy replied, taking a closer look at me.

"Don't worry. I'm in control," I told her. "Sort of... I think." I knew I owed her more of an explanation, but didn't have anything else to offer. I didn't know what the problem was. "Look, I'm not worried about hurting you. It's just not there. The motivation, feeling, anything."

"I'm not worried either," she said after a short pause. "But, I think you might want to figure out what's going on before it gets much worse."

For the first time in weeks I relaxed. Until I told Kathy about them, my intrusive thoughts were an apparition, an entity that existed solely in my head. Once she knew, that changed. They were out in the open, public property so to speak. Better still, neither of us was afraid of them. The shift in mentality was a relief. It also emphasized how much impact the thoughts were having on me.

It felt good to reveal my strange thoughts to Kathy. I felt less like a victim, but knew that wouldn't last if I didn't find out what was causing them. So, I went back to my deliberations. Where were they coming from? No matter how far I went, I always came back to the same place... combat. The violent thoughts had to be related to the most violent part of my life.

Once the connection between intrusive thoughts and war was established, it seems logical that I would have gone right to the conclusion that Post Traumatic Stress Disorder was playing a role in what was going on in my head, but that's not the case.

- 2 -

When I left the army in 1970, Post Traumatic Stress Disorder didn't exist as a term, and wouldn't make the news for quite a few years. All I knew about combat related psychological disorders came from movies and television. They called it "shell shock" and "combat fatigue."

Invariably, the victims in the shows lost control in the middle of a battle, broke down, and ended up in the psychiatric ward. The stereotypical characters were depicted as weak, defective, or both. Like most young men I wasn't terribly empathetic because I couldn't see myself loosing it like that. In Vietnam I got to prove what I felt about myself was true.

Distinguished Flying Cross Award

When a friendly company made contact with an unknown size enemy force in bunkers and trees, they requested and received the support of an aerial scout team to assist in their maneuver. During the active exchange of fire, Warrant Officer Smith, flying at tree top level, relayed key information of enemy locations for tactical fighter air strikes, and even though his reconnaissance mission was completed, he voluntarily offered his assistance to the ground commander in order to evacuate two seriously wounded soldiers. With great skill, Warrant Officer Smith maneuvered his aircraft to a location where the wounded could be lifted onto the aircraft. Before the second man could be placed on the ship, they began receiving fire from snipers. Without regard for his own safety Warrant Officer Smith remained at a low hover

while his gunner and ground troops placed
suppressive fire into the trees so that the second
soldier could be loaded onto the ship. His
outstanding...

There's no denying I was very uncomfortable when the
guys in the trees began shooting at us. If I'd had enough time I
might have crapped in my pants when a B-40 rocket missed us by
a few feet. Nevertheless, it was pretty obvious to me that I had
what it takes to make it through a fight without losing control.

PTSD didn't exist and I couldn't relate to people with
psychological issues from war, but stories began circulating among
my veteran friends about guys with problems. Having fought hard
with no apparent side effects, it was difficult for me to understand
exactly what the trouble was. It would have sounded like whining
if the veterans I heard about weren't combat infantry types. It made
sense that a few of those guys would lose it. They saw some awful
things. But it really didn't matter what I thought or how I felt, I
was with them. We were all part of an insignificant war no one
wanted.

A number of years later a guy shot someone and told the
press he'd been having "flashbacks," that being in Vietnam had
screwed him up. I felt betrayed. It wasn't just that he'd committed
a crime and was using combat as an excuse. To blame that type of
behavior on what we did as combatants belittled the rest of us,
even those who died. He had taken our tarnished war to a new
low... and I was proud of what I'd done as a soldier.

I learned how to fly helicopters, a monumental
accomplishment for me at the time, and spent most of my tour of
duty as a scout pilot for the 1st Cavalry Division. Like military
scouts through history my job was to locate the enemy.

I flew the OH-6 Hughes Cayuse, an extremely responsive
and forgiving machine. With a Minigun that I controlled from the
cockpit mounted on the left side of the fuselage, and a door gunner
with his M-60 machine gun behind me in the open passenger
compartment on the right side, it was also very deadly.

To find the North Vietnamese soldiers in the dense jungle
we flew low and slow, 30 or 40 miles an hour right down in the
tops of the trees, doing tight turns and circles to follow the trails

—

9

they used. When we caught up to them they were waiting, hidden in the jungle right below us, so close we could see their faces and the weapons in their hands when they stood up and began shooting.

Being a scout was dangerous, but rewarding. We worked directly with the grunts: the guys on the ground doing the dirty work. We helped them find the bunker complexes they were always looking for, and avoid ambushes along the way. When they made contact with the enemy, we put down suppressive fire and gave them information on the guys they were fighting. Often we directed artillery from the fire support bases and marked targets for Navy and Air Force bombs. And when things got bad, we helped them find the way out. At the end of the day, the sense of accomplishment almost outweighed the overwhelming fatigue.

My life in the air was demanding, rewarding, and on the ground it was surprisingly simple. When I climbed out of that aircraft I didn't have a lot to worry about, or concerns of any nature, relatively speaking. There were few norms or traditions, no relevant past or foreseeable future, only staying alive.

Life was oddly balanced… right up to my last day with the 1st Cavalry, when I was shot down for the second time and seriously injured. There was a lot of pain and discomfort, but several months later I was feeling fine.

The first day they let me off the grounds of Walter Reed Army Medical Center, I got on a local bus to Bethesda on the outskirts of Washington D.C. Along the way I stopped at a Salvation Army store and bought a pair of nearly new blue jeans and a few clean button-down-collar shirts.

I didn't feel like spending my hard earned money on shiny new civilian clothes; too much like a uniform. Then I caught another bus to the Porsche dealer in Bethesda and wrote them a check for a brand new silver 911T Targa.

That beautiful car cost almost every dollar I'd made in Vietnam, which I thought was appropriate. As well as a reward, it represented the final step in the process of leaving my military career behind. The Porsche was, literally, the vehicle that was going to take me into the flow of civilian life. It seemed to me, with a ride like that, there were going to be a lot of good times ahead.

Once I had my car, instead of lamenting my situation as a

---

patient in a military hospital, I looked forward to every minute of the coming day. After breakfast I was in my 911 heading out of the city. The back roads of Virginia, the Shenandoah Valley and West Virginia were where I spent the rest of my day.

It was spring, roof-off weather, and it didn't take long for those ambling drives to become the center of my life. The car was comfortable, the controls felt good in my hands and I liked the perspective, constant change, glimpses of places and times. I was reestablishing contact with the "real world," as we'd called it, from a comfortable distance.

When they released me from the hospital I moved in with a friend while the Army processed my discharge papers. His girlfriend had a drug problem and a dog. A few days after I officially separated from active duty she left town a little ahead of the police. The next day my friend went looking for her and I was left with Zach, the biggest Doberman pinscher I'd ever met.

I didn't know much about the large black and brown dog with gleaming front teeth that were at least two inches long. The girl said she'd given him drugs, but it didn't show. If anything his composure bordered on aloofness. Anyway, there wasn't anything to keep me where I was so I packed my duffle bag, got in the 911, opened the passenger's door and said to Zach, "Want to go for a ride?"

Somewhere in central Pennsylvania the sun came out and the Targa's roof came off. I was on my way home in my beautiful Porsche; completely free for the first time in years, I realized with a surge of good feelings. As far as I knew, I'd never been happier. I looked at Zach and felt like sharing. The only thing that came to mind was a happy howl. On the second one, with a little more feeling, the big dog joined in, deep and soulful, with his large nose raised to the blue sky above. That's when I knew we were going to be good friends.

At the end of the day we were deep in the mountains of Upstate New York, in a house I'd known since childhood. I spent almost every summer of my life in the brook out front, hopping rocks, swimming in the deep, cold pools, and lying in the sun on the warm boulders to dry, the scent of warm pine needles always in the air. If driving was a sanctuary for me, my home in the mountains was Shangri-La.

The property I owned with my brothers and sister not far from Keene Valley was large enough to be private, and the people in the small town had known me long enough not to be too interested in what I was doing. Which was good. I didn't want any outside influences in my life. My first thought of the day was... no need to think. Then I did whatever came next.

Usually it was a walk in the woods with Zach. While I walked three miles, he ran twenty. The big dog was never gone more than a few minutes at a time and always knew where I was. I couldn't lose him, and when I sat down to enjoy a spot he'd sit with his back to mine, keeping an eye on the area I couldn't see. I don't know if he was doing that for me, or both of us. The rest of the day I spent working around the house. With all the land and a fairly old building, there were an endless number of relatively simple jobs to keep me busy.

For a few months, working in the sun and Zach's company were all I needed. However, at the end of the day I liked a drink or two. I didn't mind drinking alone, but it didn't make much sense when there was a great bar, the Elm Tree Inn, just down the road.

Their homemade soups came with a pad of butter melting in the center, the steaks were thick and juicy, and the company diverse and entertaining. I'd known the owners, Monty Purdy and his son Ron, most of my life.

Before long I was there every evening, often spending four or five hours at the bar, coming home drunk around one or two in the morning. Towards the end of summer most of the people I'd been drinking with left town for college or jobs in the city. My social life came to a screeching halt, but not the time I spent in the Elm Tree.

The bar was three miles from the speed limit sign in Keene Valley, and I could get there in less than two minutes. I liked to drive fast. I had to be right there, prepared for the unexpected to happen quickly. It required my full attention.

I enjoyed the challenge. Focusing intently on one thing felt good. However, increasingly, particularly when I was drunk, I felt compelled to go faster. The closer I got to the edge, where there was absolutely no room for error, the more in control I felt. I knew it wasn't smart, that the odds were against me, but I was use to operating in that environment.

I believed I could handle the drinking and driving, but I knew it was going to get me in trouble. Every couple of months I got another speeding ticket. I could also see that I was spending too much time at the bars in the area, getting drunk earlier in the day and staying that way. However, I chose to ignore the issue until one night around closing time at the Elm Tree, when I came very close to getting the shit beaten out of me by some rednecks because I was wearing combat boots.

The next morning I couldn't understand why they'd want to pound on a vet for wearing his boots, until I remembered what an asshole I'd been. How I kept getting louder, telling people what I thought, which was apparently offensive to some, until a guy with only a couple teeth in his mouth began making fun of me and my boots. If not for Ron, he would have beaten me up.

I was embarrassed and didn't want to go to the bar that night, or the next, and decided to take a drive. My brother Peter was working on his Master's degree in nuclear engineering at the University of Denver, the same college that suspended me right before I got drafted. He called and said there was a big party that weekend and lots of my friends were going to be there. I mixed up a gallon of strong tea, got Zach in the 911 and drove 2,000 miles to Denver.

I drove fast, between 90 and 110 mph, honing my ability to detect speed traps and the highway patrols. Driving all night and into the next day was a marathon, not like the comfortable trips I took from Walter Reed Army Medical Center.

When Zach and I got back from our trip to Denver it was cold in the mountains of Upstate New York, and there wasn't much to do. We even dropped our walks in the woods when hunting season began.

The sound of a gunshot anywhere near made me fearful, angry. I could see the slug leave the hunter's rifle on its way through the woods, nicking leaves, barely missing limbs and trees, on a course to the side of my head. I knew the odds were astronomical, but it also made sense. After all the bullets that had been fired at me and missed, it seemed absurdly appropriate that a hunter's random shot would blow my brains out.

I knew why I reacted to the sound of a gunshot the way I did, and it didn't bother me, but I'd begun to have night sweats. Sometimes I'd sweat so much in my sleep the sheet would be sopping wet. There were also reoccurring nightmares. One in particular bothered me.

It always began and ended in the same place. I'm in the back of a Huey cruising low level over the jungle. There's no noise or action, I'm just sitting on the bench seat looking forward as both of the pilots lose consciousness.

Almost immediately the aircraft begins a slow roll to the right, dropping towards the tops of the trees not that far below. I know I have to get to the controls in a matter of seconds or we'll die. But, when I try to move, I can't. It's as if I'm mired in mud. Slowly I force an arm forward and struggle to follow, but I know I won't get to the controls in time. That's when I wake up, muscles tense and heart pounding.

The nightmare bothered me. The feeling of not being able to save myself was incredibly frustrating. And the way it kept coming up over and over again, I figured it had to be related to something problematic. However, I didn't spend much time thinking about it. I gave up on psycho-evaluations when I was a teenager.

The school I was going to at the time recommended that I see a psychiatrist because I was constantly in trouble. One minute

I'd be standing around with friends, doing what kids do, and the next minute I'd be in front of some authority figure explaining myself. I was the kid who always got caught.

The psychiatrist's last report to my parents concluded that I had no significant psychological issues, but believed that I had a problem seeing the consequence of my actions, which made sense to me. It was hard to have fun and be responsible at the same time. He also thought I saw things just one way, my own, but not for the sake of ego or defiance. He inferred it was actually a perception issue. I thought he was making a lot out of very little and, overall, felt that psychiatry was a guessing game for bored people.

I didn't need a psychiatrist to tell me where the fear of getting shot by a hunter, or the night sweats and nightmares came from. They were a consequence of going to war, and I could live with that. What other choice did I have? Anyway, I knew that it was a small price to pay compared to what a lot of guys were going through.

It seemed that most of my good friends from Vietnam were having problems with their wives or girlfriends. One had wrecked his trophy Corvette, several had lost their licenses, and one was dead. His pickup went off a cliff on the way home in the middle of the night. The guy who told me about it believed his death wasn't an accident.

So why feel bad about a few infrequent and inconsequential irregularities. Besides, there were signs of improvement. Some time before the road trip to Denver I stopped sleeping with a loaded gun by my bed.

As fall became winter, the last signs of life in the valley disappeared. At night the long scraggly limbs of the barren trees along the side of the road looked threatening as they flashed in and out of my headlights. Everything seemed lifeless, from the gray road in front of me to the dark shapes of the mountains against the starless sky. Even the Elm Tree Inn was dead. People sat at the bar alone or talked in low tones at tables.

My state of mind began to resemble my environment, lifeless. More and more often I felt out of sync with the people around me. Most of the time it seemed to be my problem, as if I were missing something. Sometimes it felt like rejection. The net effect was less interaction and more time at home by myself.

15

When I did go out it wasn't as much fun. No one seemed to have a sense of humor, and I was tired of talking about serious subjects like the war. What we did over there was no longer open to debate. People could have their opinions, but I wasn't about to let anyone tell me what was right or wrong with a war they didn't fight.

As my mindset changed so did my outlook on life. Instead of getting up feeling like I was part of the day, I felt detached, listless, in a fog. My energy was gone, and so was my patience. Before long Zach was drawn into my bad moods. I'd yell at him and throw him out of the house. Although I was convinced that it was his fault, I'm not a mean person and knew I was mistreating my loyal friend, especially when I drank too much.

My life was changing. I could feel the imbalance. It felt like a series of bad days more than anything else, until one evening as I sat in front of the fire sipping a glass of bourbon with Zach.

I looked out the window to my left. The light was almost gone. I could barely make out the far side of the clearing. For no apparent reason I began to feel uneasy. Confused, I continued to stare. Then, like a squall crossing open water something swept over me and was gone, leaving behind a sense of helplessness, vulnerability.

It took a moment, but I recognized the sensation for what it was, a common depression. The type I got when things went regrettably wrong. Surprisingly, it was the first time since Vietnam that I'd felt anything like that. In fact, I realized that the only time I was remotely depressed in combat was at the beginning of my tour of duty; before I came to the realization that, if I wasn't wounded or dead, things were going well.

When I went on to consider why I was depressed, the reason was right in front of my face... the weather. It figured that the cold, gray winter months had finally brought me down, and I decided it was time for a major change. Zach came over with a look of concern, sat and put his head on my leg. "Ever been on an airplane?" I asked.

My choice for a reprieve from the winter weather was St. Croix, an island in the Caribbean Sea. It had been home from the time I was ten until my parents died in a plane crash on a neighboring island seven years later. Other than their deaths, the island had good memories.

As kids we went everywhere on horses, riding bareback with the tether rope for a bridal. If my brothers and I weren't in school or doing chores for dad, we were in the water. Miles of white sand beaches, perfect body surfing waves, and not another person in sight.

However, in hindsight, St. Croix probably wasn't the best place to go for relaxation. The tropics were a good idea. I always felt better in sunny places. But after the massacre at a golf course on the north shore of the island, where a daylight robbery by several black men turned really ugly, the small, easy-going white community became understandably leery.

As burglaries became increasingly common around the island and acts of violence, although sporadic, were extremely brutal, homes became armed camps. Everyone was carrying guns when I got there. Within days I was too.

Exposure to the hostility and fear on the island wasn't good for me. Although I had a weapon around most of the time, I couldn't relax. Occasionally I was frightened, but mostly I couldn't get away from an uncomfortable level of alertness.

To make things worse, a life-long friend of mine on the island, Pat, had a brother who was pretty crazy. While Pat and his wife, Patty, were at my place for dinner one night, Pat's brother killed their parents and then went looking for his brothers.

The police caught up with him before he found out Pat was

at my house, so there was no threat; however, when I realized how close we'd come to having a madman walk in on us with a shotgun, instead of feeling fortunate, I felt irrationally irresponsible.

Several weeks later Zach and I were at Pat and Patty's apartment. Patty had offered to cut my hair and I'd brought a six-pack. Sitting shirtless on a kitchen chair, concentrating on holding my head steady for Patty, my gaze was fixed on the couch across the room.

Beside the lamp on an end table was Pat's holstered revolver. Unlike the fantasy I'd have later with Kathy and the knife, I didn't see myself committing a violent act. I simply thought about picking the pistol up and pulling the trigger until the chambers were empty.

The thought was a surprise more than anything. It didn't freak me out like the vision of stabbing Kathy in the back would later; however, it was bizarre enough to warrant moving on to something else. Later, when I had a chance to reflect on the incident, I decided it was probably related to all the recent violence in my life.

When it was springtime in the Adirondack Mountains I went home to a feeling of peace and security. A few months later the summer people came back and the good times picked up right where they'd left off. As fall approached I decided that, rather than try to ride out winter again, I'd go back to college.

It wasn't just the thought of another long, dark, cold winter alone in the mountains, drinking myself into oblivion. I was getting low on cash. Before too long I'd have to find a job. It made sense to go back to school and get a degree in something that would make a career more profitable, and the GI Bill would pay for it.

Logic aside, returning to the University of Denver was exactly the right thing to do. Every year the school brought eight thousand kids from all over the world together in the middle of a young, growing city on the edge of some of the best recreational mountains in the country. It was a great big party.

Almost everyone I'd gone to school with before I went to war was still in town. My brother was there too, so I moved into an oversized closet in the remodeled garage he called home. All his landlord had done to renovate the property was nail the car doors shut, put in a few 2x4 walls, hook up a stove and plumb a toilet.

Keene Valley had been the right place to relax after a war. But Denver was the place to reenter civilian life. Being part of an energetic college community, having so many things to do in the city and the surrounding mountains, was obviously the next step. And, surprisingly, getting good grades was relatively easy the second time around.

That summer I went back to the mountains of Upstate New York. It was nice to be home again, relaxing in the brook, getting a lot of sleep, but regrettably I managed to total my beautiful silver Porsche.

The road I took that night had great corners. It felt like the car was glued to the asphalt, but I'd had too much to drink. Only two turns from the end of the winding road it flipped and rolled over three times before coming to rest against a tree. My car was a year and a half old and had 72,000 miles on the odometer when it died.

Fortunately, I had enough sense to carry a collision policy, and my understanding insurance company, USAA, was nice enough to buy me another 911... after cautioning, that if I got another DWI, they would discontinue my coverage.

My grades began to drop when I went back to the University of Denver in the fall. All of my courses were going down together, which lead me to believe the problem was related to attitude, not ability. So I took the winter semester off. With some money my Grandmother sent me, I bought a used 4x4 canvas-top Bronco, outfitted it for living on the beach, and headed south with Zach, my constant companion.

We made our way to the far side of the Yucatan Peninsula and camped on a deserted beach among some palm trees for a few months before heading back to Colorado for spring skiing at Vail. Then it was back to Upstate New York for the summer, where my second Porsche ended up totaled against an enormous pine tree. I wasn't in the car at the time. I had actually encouraged a friend with whom I'd been drinking to take it for a drive, as fast as he wanted to go.

Even though I had collision coverage, and there were no tickets involved, I decided not to get another Porsche. For one thing, I couldn't afford the insurance premiums. For another, over

---

19

the past few months I'd gotten the feeling I might die in the car. Nothing purposeful, just something that was going to happen.

My fast driving days were over, but the idea of drinking less never crossed my mind. Bars were my primary source of social contact, and I enjoyed drinking. The first glass of bourbon on ice was relaxing. The second always had that subtle exhilaration. Somewhere in the third drink I usually got the distinct impression that things were about to get interesting. Invariably they did.

In the fall I went to a friend's wedding not far from home. That's where I met Darcie. She was very perceptive and direct. I enjoyed her company and we spent the rest of the weekend together. With nothing better to do, I followed her to New York where she was working as a publicist, but after two days I was ready to get out of the city. There wasn't anything to do that didn't cost a ridiculous amount of money, and the streets were windy and cold. Even Central Park was depressing.

When I got home it was decision time. The weather in the mountains was deteriorating fast. The question wasn't if, but where to go. I decided against going back to school because I didn't want to flunk out again. So looking for work was the only other option, which meant flying. I didn't know how to do anything else.

I decided on California. I'd heard that, other than the Gulf of Mexico and Alaska, two extreme places, the west coast was the only place where there were any jobs. A few days before I was going to leave, Darcie called. When I told her that Zach and I were on our way west to look for work, she asked if she could come along.

Part of the trip included a detour to the Baja where we joined my brothers Peter, Nulsen and Van for Christmas. After a couple weeks of camping on the beach and drinking tequila, Darcie, Zach and I ended up in Oxnard, California. Work was scarce because of the surplus of helicopter pilots from Vietnam, so I took the first offer I got, a job in Indonesia.

Aviation Management Company of Salt Lake City hired thirty pilots and flew us to Jakarta on the island of Java. From there I went to work on the island of Borneo, which was on the exact opposite side of the world from Zach and Darcie.

It was a unique experience, meeting people who'd never seen a helicopter, or a white man, but I missed Darcie and my dog and returned to California as soon as my contract allowed. I wanted to settle down. Not have kids or anything like that, just stay in one place for a while, relax and enjoy being in California.

I got what I wanted, my dog, girlfriend and a regular job flying a helicopter from an airport not far from our house near the beach. I even bought an old wooden sailboat for a couple hundred dollars and, after sanding and varnishing for a year, had her looking good and sailing well.

Things had changed quite a bit since I met Darcie. I felt like my life had purpose, was more interesting. When she suggested a vacation in Hawaii, which would be a good place to be married, I was all for it. We had a simple wedding on a beach in Honolulu and went back to California the next day.

Several months later Zach died of cancer. I'd never felt that kind of loss, or cried so hard. My parents were different; as were the people I knew who died in Vietnam.

Not long after my best friend's death I was flying down the coast past Rincon and noticed an oddly colored mudslide. It was bright orange, flowing right down the main, and only, street of Sea Cliff.

When I pulled into the carport that evening, I noticed the same color mud on the side of Darcie's car. Later that night I casually mentioned that I knew she'd been in Sea Cliff that day. I thought I was being clever, that she'd be curious and want to know how I knew, but that wasn't the case.

"You sneaky little son-of-a-bitch," she hissed. "That's right, I'm balling Rick, and I want a divorce!" Then she got up and walked out of the house. Rick was a coach at the tennis club we belonged to, who I'd just found out lived in Sea Cliff. A second later the door opened and Darcie's head appeared. "Don't you dare cancel our membership!" she told me in a menacing tone, and left again.

I had no idea what had been going on, which was hard for most of my friends to believe. It turned out that Rick was the latest lover on a long list, including bag boys at the market, a car salesman, the guy who installed the outdoor Jacuzzi, quite a few of my friends, and one of my brothers when we were camping in

22

Mexico.

The fact that Darcie was less than a perfect wife didn't diminish the impact of her leaving. Through no apparent fault of my own, life as I knew it was over. My attempt to settle down had failed. I felt cheated, used, confused, saddened by the breach of trust, and angry with myself for letting it happen.

Within days of Darcy's departure I quit my job. Distracted as I was, flying night rescue missions offshore didn't seem like a good idea. A few days later I began running on the beach. Initially it was to get out of the house, away from the enclosed space and moribund thoughts, but I stuck with it for other reasons. The physical demand on my body leveled the peaks and valleys of my emotions. The metered stride and rhythmic breathing worked like a sieve sorting wheat from chaff. Superfluous thoughts became fewer and farther between, until all I had on my mind were priorities and associated facts.

Soon I was running four or five days a week. I also went out on my sailboat more often. It felt good to take the tiller and point her nose to sea, feel the land drop away and leave everything behind.

Chiquita was 28 feet on the deck, had a narrow beam and soft curve to her double-ended stern. She was made entirely of wood, cedar over oak, solid. Soon I was sailing her on the windiest days because I'd found that, when the lee rail was buried and I could barely see the oncoming waves through the briny spray off her bow, I felt good. A lot like driving fast but less likely to crash and die... or so I thought.

One afternoon it was blowing 25 mph, gusting over 30. I was drinking schnapps off the neck, close hauled on a beam reach, loving every second of it, but kept the lee chain plates under water too long. I knew they leaked, but didn't realize how much until the bow went into a breaking three-foot swell and didn't come out the other side.

Green water raced over the forward hatch, up the slope of the cabin and into the cockpit before I could move. For the longest time the boat felt as if she was on her way to the bottom, then she shuddered and rose out of the turbulent sea. When I looked down the companionway the water was two feet deep in the cabin. That's what had almost pulled Chiquita and me under.

I had my distractions, but every time I thought about Darcie the floor dropped out from under me. I couldn't believe how naïve I'd been. Her affairs didn't bother me nearly as much as letting the charade continue as long as it had. By being so stupid, I felt like an accomplice, that I had helped her set me up.

Sometime within the first week or two after Darcie left, a neighbor came by. We didn't have a lot in common. He was a lawyer for the county and a pretty serious individual; however, he caught me at a low time and was someone to talk to.

When I told him about the problem I was having getting over Darcie, he said, "It's like a loop, right? Every time you think of her the same thoughts come up over and over again."

"Yeah," I agreed. "It's really ridiculous. How long does it take to get past that?" I knew that he had gone through a rough divorce several years earlier.

"The rest of your life if you let it," he said, staring at me intently. "Here's what you do. As soon as you think about her, as soon as those repetitive thoughts come up, envision a tape recorder inside you. You know, the old kind with the buttons like piano keys. When you think about her the tape starts playing. That's the loop, right?" His voice became stern. "Now listen, when it starts to play. When the loop begins, see yourself reach in and push the stop button."

"That's it?" I asked, wondering where you put a tape recorder inside yourself. "Just reach in and push the button on an imaginary tape recorder?"

"Try it," he insisted. "And remember, you're the only one who can do anything about it. The one who can stop it."

I closed my eyes and pictured Darcie. Sure enough I felt my stomach muscles tighten. Knowing well what was coming next

I did as the lawyer suggested, envisioned a portable recorder and pushed the stop key. Through the little plastic window I saw the tape slide to a halt and, surprisingly, felt myself relax. It was weird.

Within days I had control of the loop Darcie usually put me in. She wasn't out of my head by any stretch of the imagination, but I could let her go at will. Once I got past that point life began to look better. I even saw how lucky I was the relationship hadn't lasted longer. But there was one nagging question. How likely was it that the same thing would happen again? I'd been so gullible for so long, I had to be missing something.

Even though I had little respect for psychiatrists and their cookie-cutter solutions, I figured that someone who specialized in divorces would be interesting to talk to and might have some useful insights. I made an appointment with a guy I picked out of the phone book. After a brief history of my life and what I was looking for from him, I asked the psychiatrist what he thought.

"Well," he began, and hesitated. "It's hard for me to say."

"What do you mean?" I asked.

"I mean," he continued. "I don't have a problem advising you on the divorce part of it. You're doing fine. You have a good lawyer and aren't contesting anything. You've accepted both your roles in this. You're also in a fine position to get on with your life." He paused again. "What I'm having a problem with is relating to you." When I didn't react, he continued. "If I'm correct, you did ask for an assessment of your ability to make decisions. Particularly in the matter of women and long-term relationships."

"Yes, I did," I assured him.

"Well, that's where I have a problem," he paused and looked out the window. "You see, I grew up right here in Ventura, went to college, got my degree in psychiatry and went right to work." For a moment I thought he was done. "I've been sitting here listening to you. The things you've done. And I'm thinking, why is this guy still alive?" He sighed. "To be honest I don't have the slightest idea how a mind like yours works, much less how you will react in a hypothetical situation."

I considered what he'd said, and asked half joking, "You think I'm crazy?"

The psychiatrist laughed. "Clinically? No." Then he paused for a moment, weighing his words. "Actually... yes, because

26

putting yourself in harm's way as often as you do is not rational. From Vietnam to..."

"No fair," I exclaimed. "Vietnam was a war. I..."

"But why scouts?" he asked, interrupting me in turn.

"Because it..." I was about to say, because it was great flying, but that seemed a little ridiculous. "I see what you mean," I conceded.

"I believe you're impulsive, no doubt, and a risk taker," he concluded, hastily adding. "But risk takers are an integral part of society. Without them not much would change."

I could see where he got the impression I took unnecessary risks, but I didn't like being told I was impulsive. Other than drinking and driving, nearly every unsafe thing I did was related to work, which involved calculated risks, not impulsive acts. I didn't try to explain that to the doctor because, as he said, he was having a hard time relating to me.

The psychiatrist ended the session by telling me I'd probably learned a valuable lesson from Darcie, and was perfectly capable of making decisions related to marriage. "They're not all like her," he said with a smile that didn't last long.

Two months after Darcie left it was time to go. I was running out of money and there was no reason to stay. My old job was out of the question. The only person I had anything in common with was the chief pilot. We'd both screwed my wife. So I called my best friend from the army, Craig, who didn't hesitate to offer me a job.

7

Craig and I met walking penalty laps on the basketball court behind the barracks. I think it was the first or second day of flight school. After our punishment, which ran longer than usual because we got caught talking, we had a beer together. Other than his clear blue eyes and a long pale scar down his right temple, Craig seemed like a pretty normal guy, but he was a little different.

He spoke in incomplete sentences; sometimes without a beginning, other times without an end, but always mumbled in an unintelligible southern drawl. However, once I learned to interpret, I found that his wit was both subtle and hilarious. Another thing I liked about him was that he had very little respect for authority.

Craig offered me a job when I called from California because we'd been best friends since flight school, and because it was payback of sorts. Without my assistance he wouldn't have his job.

Not long after Darcie and I moved to California he dropped by looking for work. I was looking for a job too, but not very hard. Actually, if not for The Palms, a nearby bar, I wouldn't have been able to say I was looking for work at all.

Flying jobs opened and closed quickly. I'd learned that without a phone it was almost impossible to get hired. Our apartment didn't have a telephone, but there was one behind the bar at The Palms. After establishing myself as a dependable customer, the bartender let me leave the number for work-related calls.

One hot afternoon while Craig and I were having a beer, the bartender came over with the phone in his hand. "Some guy named Dick lookin' for you. You here?" When I shrugged, he handed me the phone, adding, "I think he figured out I ain't your secretary."

"Mr. Smith? This is Dick Hall, chief pilot here at Brilles Rotor and Wing, and I have your resume in front of me. We're looking for pilots to work in Bolivia on a six-months-on, one-month-off, schedule."

"Bolivia?" I asked, buying time while I tried to remember exactly where Bolivia was.

"Yeah," he continued. You put down that you have time in a two-o-six." I knew that he was talking about a helicopter made by Bell Helicopters, but I wasn't sure which model the 206 was. "You have a hundred hours in them," he added impatiently.

That jogged my memory. Brilles was the first application I'd filled out when I began looking for work on the West coast, and I wasn't as prepared as I should have been. Halfway through the form there was a section entitled "Time as Pilot in Command", followed by a list of a dozen aircraft.

Most of the helicopters listed on the application were Bell or Hughes. I had time in some of the aircraft they made; however, the ones on the form were listed by their civilian names, not the military designations I was use to.

I knew that the Bell 205 listed on the application was the same as the UH-1 Huey we flew in Vietnam, and the OH-6 I flew in scouts was really a Hughes 500, but I wasn't sure of the others. Not wanting to let a job go by that I might be qualified for, I had put down a hundred hours for the aircraft I didn't recognize.

Covering the mouthpiece with my hand, I turned to Craig. "What's a two-o-six?"

"Idjit," he said, wiping foam from his upper lip. "That's a Jet Ranger."

I knew the helicopter, but I'd never flown one. "You got any time in 'em?" I asked my friend.

"Flew one last week in Arizona."

"Then you talk to this guy," I said, handing Craig the phone. A few days later he was in La Paz. The next year the operation in Bolivia shut down and Craig went to work for Tundra Copters, a company Brilles owned in Fairbanks. Soon he was their chief pilot, then general manager.

Craig and his wife Sheryl let me move in with them when I got to Fairbanks. Within days I felt more like myself than I had in

---

a long time. The environment at Tundra was incredibly relaxed. If we weren't flying or taking care of paperwork, most of us were behind the hanger sitting in the sun. When the day was done, Craig and I drank a beer or two with the other pilots and mechanics, then went home to Sheryl's fine southern cooking. Later we'd go out for a few more drinks, and occasionally get fairly drunk.

My first summer in Alaska was remarkable. The awesome stone faces of Mounts Debra, Hess and Hayes at 12,000 feet in the light of a full moon, the terror of turbulence in Windy Pass, and the peace and tranquility of the Brooks Range. I'd never seen anything like the soft pastels of the midnight sun on the North Slope, or the intense sunrises in Fairbanks at two in the morning.

The work was hard by some standards, twelve hours in the cockpit, living out of tents for months at a time, and no warm water. The flying was also a challenge. Most of the landing sites were on the slopes of steep mountains, in soft tundra bogs or among tall trees. But I liked what I did and the people I worked with, and at night I slept well.

In the fall, I went back to my house in California to spend the winter. I sailed Chiquita for a month then put her and the house up for sale. I had lost touch with that part of the world. By spring everything was sold and I was on my way back to Alaska. On final approach to Fairbanks I looked down on the meandering rivers of the Tanana Valley. What I saw was harsh and familiar. I was glad to be back.

The summer went by quickly. I flew all but a few days from March to October. When the jobs dropped off because of the cold, I went to Tahiti and lived with a fisherman and his family in a thatch and plywood hut on Bora Bora for several months. Twelve dollars a day included breakfast, lunch and dinner, which all tasted a lot like fish.

8

My third summer in Alaska I took Craig's usual job of flying for the Forest Service's Forestry Sciences Lab. It was field camp work, living in tents in remote areas for the summer, and Sheryl wanted Craig closer to home because she was pregnant.

Just before the job began, Craig told me about the people I'd be working with. One of them was Kathy. "You're gonna like her," he told me. He was right. She was independent and confident, quick-witted and liked to laugh. I even liked the way she dressed, blue jeans and flannel shirts with her long blond hair tucked into her well-worn cowboy hat. She was also very fit.

Kathy was as natural as she could be, and honest, a quality I'd learned to appreciate in a woman. We also had a lot in common, grew up in similar environments, and felt the same way about nearly everything. Before long I was flirting with her.

On the way back to camp after a long day's work in the Talkeetna Mountains, I landed at the top of a snowfield with Kathy and the members of her crew. One of the guys had a hand-cranked ice-cream maker back in camp. All we needed was a bucket full of wild blueberries, which we already had, and something to chill the ingredients.

I parked the helicopter not far from a cornice, where the snow was compacted and the helicopter wouldn't fall through. While the other people in the helicopter harvested the hard-packed snow for the ice-cream maker, Kathy and I walked to the edge of the cornice and peered over. There was a vertical drop of six or eight feet to the snowfield that ran down the steep mountainside for a couple of hundred feet.

"Wish I had my skis," Kathy commented casually.

For the record, what I did next would not have happened if

I didn't think she could handle it; and, I was going to follow her.

"Too bad you don't," I said as I gave her a little push.

She didn't scream or even curse, as might be expected. Instead Kathy turned in midair. In fact, she was smiling as she grabbed the sleeve of my still extended arm and dragged me over the edge with her. Then she laughed out loud, pulled me closer and rolled.

When we hit the snow a split second later Kathy was on top. The landing hurt. It wasn't as soft as I'd believed. And then we began accelerating at an alarming rate, which didn't bother Kathy who rode me like a sled right into the rocks and brush at the bottom of the snowfield. I was lucky to get away with just a few scratches.

That probably was flirting, but what I did a few weeks later could only be considered entrapment. The end of summer was approaching and Kathy would be on her way, but I wasn't ready to say goodbye. I'd been thinking about going to Australia or New Zealand that winter, and knew I couldn't find a better traveling companion. The plot thickened when I saw a two-for-one ticket sale, LA to Auckland on Pan American Airlines.

At the campfire after work one evening I mentioned to Kathy that I'd been to Australia and would like to see New Zealand. Her eyes widened and she told me that she had wanted to see that part of the world too, particularly New Zealand. When I told her about the Pan Am tickets, and suggested we take bicycles and camp, she thought it was a great idea.

Towards the end of October, when the flying season was over, Kathy and I loaded our bicycles in boxes and put them on an airplane with us to New Zealand. We biked up North Island then down South Island to Queenstown, where we hiked the Dart, Reese and Routeburn trails.

Our time together in New Zealand went well. There wasn't one part of the trip we didn't enjoy, even when our jet lost an engine departing Christchurch. That was okay because the airline paid our bills for two days while they put in a new engine.

When we got back to Fairbanks, Kathy began work on her Master's Degree in Wildlife Biology at the University of Alaska. With some of the money from the sale of my house in California I bought a small place near the airport and we began fixing it up.

That summer we worked for the Forest Service again. During the winter, while I slept or hung out with Craig, Kathy continued work on her degree at the university. The next summer we had to go separate ways.

Kathy went to Hinchinbrook Island for two months to do the fieldwork for her thesis while I stayed in Fairbanks to fly a forest-fire contract for the state. Although we'd been in constant company for two years, we thought two months apart was too long, so I promised Kathy I'd find a way to see her.

A month later Craig arranged a few days off while my helicopter was down for maintenance. With the help of a friend and his sailboat, I made my way to Hinchinbrook where Kathy was studying Sitka black-tailed deer.

The day I was leaving, on a grassy knoll overlooking Shelter Bay, Kathy told me that she was going to miss me. To both of our surprise, I replied, "You know, Kat, if you want to get married . . ." but stopped when I heard her make a little choking sound. "Jesus, Kathy," I exclaimed. "You're laughing."

"No, I'm not," she said, but was unable to keep it in. After Kathy regained her composure, trying to look as sincere as she could under the circumstances, she said, "I love you, Tommy. I really do. But I wasn't expecting that. I mean... well, I just don't want to get married yet." She paused, looking at me with concern, and added, "But if I did, it would be to you."

Completely embarrassed, I continued lamely, "I was just trying to let you know how I feel." Then added something to the effect that I wasn't really interested in marriage either, but would prefer that to living without her. She told me she appreciated my sentiments and would let me know if she changed her mind.

That winter Kathy changed her mind. The catalyst was her parents'. With the children gone they'd decided to sell their house, a beautiful home on the side of Lake Michigan, and move into a smaller place. Kathy figured it would be a shame to let such a nice spot for a wedding go to waste.

Two years later, with Kathy's Master's degree in hand, we sold our little house in Fairbanks and, along with the rest of the money from the sale of my house in California, bought a piece of land on Maui and began building a garage that evolved into a small house.

II

ANGER

– 9 –

I couldn't have set my life up better. Between summers in Alaska flying, winters in Hawaii playing, and a good woman to share it all with, I had what I needed to be very content. However, the opposite was true. I was angry most of the time.

It wasn't normal anger, but more a case of extreme irritation that had been growing stronger and less discriminating over the last year. Increasingly, I began losing my temper with almost everyone for little or no reason, including my passengers.

I'd never had an abundance of affection for people in general, but I usually liked my passengers. The fact that they wanted to go into the mountains in a helicopter gave us quite a bit in common. That they had confidence in what I did was another plus, and they also paid my salary.

However, when I spent weeks at a time with the same people, more and more often I found things to dislike, sources of irritation. Most of the time it wasn't anything worth complaining about, but the effect was cumulative.

In the beginning I thought it was just part of a bush pilot's mentality, the increasing awareness that your passengers will kill you if you let them. It seemed to be the nature of the work in Alaska where flying in the mountains is risky.

The rugged terrain and extreme weather conditions were always a challenge, and landing at unprepared sites was often dangerous. There was also the aircraft. Working around them is distracting. The rotor blades put out winds up to fifty miles per hour, while the five hundred horsepower turbine engine screams like a banshee and the tail rotor threatens to chop anyone who gets near it into little pieces.

With all of that going on, people get distracted and make

mistakes. Unfortunately, doing the type of work we did, those mistakes were often disastrous and occasionally fatal. Subsequently, the longer I flew in Alaska, the less I tolerated ineptness, inexperience or any excuse for making mistakes.

Most bush pilots get that way after awhile, so the steady increase in animosity towards my passengers seemed acceptable, until Bob and Nattie. Bob and Nattie were two dedicated anthropologists from California who came to the Lime Hills to look for brachiopods.

The first day in camp it poured and they didn't have raincoats. Their excuse was acceptable. Nattie explained that they'd been so preoccupied with the research part of the trip they forgot to pack clothes. So I lent them my emergency foul weather gear, extra-large plastic trash bags with head and armholes cut to fit.

After a briefing on the do's and don'ts of helicopters I took them to a mountain loaded with the 250 million year-old, ocean-dwelling brachiopods. The band of limestone they were looking for was at 6,000 feet in mostly vertical terrain, and the only possible landing spot near the fossil-rich area was a sharp shoulder of the mountain.

I tried a normal landing, lengthwise, but rocks on the spine of the ridge threatened to puncture the belly of the aircraft, so I balanced the helicopter across the narrow ridge. Although we were teetering like a seesaw, it was relatively safe.

When I nodded, Bob and Nattie climbed out and began unloading as quickly as they could. One of the first things was the water. They had brought along half a dozen plastic containers of water because wet fossils are easier to identify. It brings out the detail. Nattie pulled one of the two-gallon containers out of the back and passed it to Bob who, as he'd been told in the preflight briefing, put the cargo in front of the helicopter where I could see it.

The slope of the ground was steep. As soon as he put the container down, it began to roll. Unfortunately, Bob didn't notice because he'd gone to get another one. The plastic container was square, so at first it just flopped from one side to the next. As the slope of the mountain increased, it picked up speed and began to bounce. A couple of feet the first time, a few more the next, and it

---

began to leak.

Before long, the container was vaulting high in the air, spewing jets of water in every direction. It was an impressive show. Then Bob put the second container down without noticing the first was gone, and went back for another as the second container began its trip down the mountainside.

I did what I could to get their attention, which wasn't much. I couldn't let go of the controls with the helicopter balanced on the ridge. But I yelled at them, rocked the helicopter up and down, wagged my head back and forth, but they didn't notice. This wasn't their fault.

The situation would be distracting for seasoned passengers, much less two absent-minded professors from the lower forty-eight. So I watched, and then began to laugh at the spectacle, as one container after the other went bounding down the three-thousand-foot slope.

When I came back for them that afternoon it was drizzling, and I had another laugh at the sight of the two trash-bag-clad figures waiting for me. However, once I had the helicopter balanced across the ridge again, humor turned to horror. As Bob and Nattie began loading their fossils into the baggage compartment, the helicopter's tail began to drop.

Once again, it wasn't their fault. In my preflight briefing, I told them to put things like rocks in the baggage compartment behind the passenger compartment, assuming they'd be loading with the landing gear flat on the ground.

Balanced on the ridge, however, that much weight so far behind the rotor mast was moving the center of gravity towards the tail. In a matter of seconds I was running out of forward control and couldn't keep the helicopter level. Even if I took off, the helicopter wouldn't fly.

Adrenalin began to flow as I tightened my grip on the controls. I knew I was only moments away from following the water containers down the mountain. Then Nattie climbed in the front seat, unwittingly counter-balancing the weight in the baggage compartment. I was to blame for what had happened, but I was so mad I couldn't look at either of them on the flight back to camp. I hated them.

I finally forgave Bob and Nattie. I couldn't hold them

responsible for doing exactly what I'd told them to do; however, it took days.

That incident was the beginning of a trend of excessive anger. There was always a reason. It usually had to do with work. Anything from leaving a greasy handprint on a Plexiglas window, to trying to make decisions only I was qualified to decide. No matter what it was, I took it personally. One minute I'd be normal, and the next I'd be furious. It seemed as though I was using my passengers' mistakes, even the potential for error, as an excuse to get angry.

A few months after Bob and Nattie, I was in the Alaska Range with a geologist from the University of Alaska. We'd been working out of Farewell Lake Lodge at the north entrance to Rainy Pass for a couple of weeks. Kathy and I had been apart for almost a month, and I was more irritable than usual.

I lost my temper over something small and came down on the poor guy like a ton of bricks. Unjustifiable as the assault was, my timing was even worse. Just a few days earlier his wife had died. I still feel like shit about that.

Problems with my temper continued to crop up more and more often, but I didn't know what to do. No one seemed to notice it but me. Neither Kathy nor Craig brought it up. I wasn't happy about the change in my disposition but was willing to ignore it if everyone else was, until I intentionally sideswiped a parked pickup truck.

Kathy was out of town for a week in Anchorage, and I was out drinking with friends until the bars closed. On the way back to the hanger the road went by the headquarters of a company I disliked.

Instead of hiring locally, they brought people in to do jobs Alaskans could do. They overcharged for shoddy work and couldn't care less about the impact they had on the state or its environment. As I drove by rows of new cars and trucks, in a rush of indignant anger, I swerved into the parking lot and sideswiped a fancy pickup.

The next morning I cringed when I remembered what I'd done. It was an unprovoked, violent, criminal act. For a while I lay in bed trying to go back to sleep, but couldn't and drove to the scene of the crime to see how much damage I'd done.

I had a note to slip under the vehicles windshield wiper that stated something to the effect that while turning into the parking lot my hand slipped on the wheel and I sideswiped their truck. I'd also written down my phone number. But I couldn't find the truck anywhere. I thought about going to the receptionist in the lobby, but not for long.

Driving home, for the first time since I'd come back from war, I truly understood how different I was. Defenseless in the face of a severe hangover, I saw myself as out of control, angry and lashing out indiscriminately. I also felt an undeniable urge to leave Alaska.

The many moves I'd made before invariably had something too do with work or recreation, but I just wanted to leave and not come back. Burnout, I told myself, too much for too long. It was time to try year-round living in Hawaii, I decided, and began making plans with a sense of purpose.

The day Kathy got back from Anchorage, I asked, "What do you think about spending next summer in Hawaii?"

"No Alaska next year at all?" she returned.

"That's what I was thinking."

"I don't know," she said, pensively. "I sure do like it here in the summer." She paused. "And the money's good. What will we do for work?"

"I can fly tours," I told her.

"That's going to get pretty boring, you know."

"We can always come back," I assured her.

"Okay," she said with a smile.

10

The residents of Maui say their island is "no ka oi," the best one. Of course the people on Oahu, Kauai, and the Big Island say something similar, and they are all correct.

The Hawaiian Islands have more of everything than any other group of tropical islands I've been to. Volcanoes that rise right out of the ocean, barren lava fields, lush tropical rainforests, waterfalls that drop for thousands of feet to the sea, long white beaches with perfect boogie board waves, and trade-winds to keep everything cool... truly nature's paradise.

I went to work flying tours out of Kaanapali Airport, a single strip of asphalt just above the high-tide line of a deserted beach. Other than a small A-frame structure that served as the terminal for the twin-engine plane that flew in and out twice a day, and an aluminum trailer that was our office, there was nothing but sugarcane fields.

It was a hot place most of the time and the company we worked for didn't want the pilots hanging around the air-conditioned office. To keep us out of the way, they let us take a golf cart across the runway to the beach where we'd swim and lie around in the sand until there was a flight.

When the pager went off, it was time to get back to the office, rinse off in the outdoor shower and go fly. After the last flight of the day we all got together in the bar above the terminal. The building was small, but because it was an A-frame, the bar was even smaller, almost claustrophobic. However, the company was good, the beer ice cold, and the bartender, High-School Harry, was among the best.

While I was working Kathy had to stay home. We only had one car. She kept busy with projects like building a stone retaining wall. When it was done, it was eighty feet long, two feet wide, three feet tall, and the average stone weighed forty or fifty pounds. It kept her in good shape, but she got lonely.

"I didn't want him either," Kathy admitted when she brought the large, ugly puppy home. She called him Mo, which was short for Slow Mo because he was so relaxed. Then she told me how she'd been by the pound several times and he was always asleep. "But the last time he was up and followed me everywhere. When I stopped, he'd sit on my foot and look up at me. It turns out they were going to put him down." She laughed. "He may be ugly and slow, but he's not stupid."

We enjoyed living in the middle of a pasture on the side of a volcano in Hawaii with our dog. The days were warm, the nights peaceful, and we had fresh papayas for breakfast. Work was fun and when we weren't working we played. I rarely thought about how much things had changed since we'd left Alaska, but when I did, I assumed that feeling better was just part of living on Maui and its relaxed environment.

Life was better, but time was working against me. In less than a year I left the company at Kaanapali after a falling out with the manager. I'd known him for five or six years and, after he agreed to pay me right back, didn't think twice about lending him 2,000 dollars for the down payment on a car. Two months later, after quitting and threatening legal action, he finally repaid the loan.

I quit because I believed it was the only way to get my money back, and because of what I thought my boss might be capable of. He had been so strange through the whole thing, like it wasn't happening, I began to think he was capable of anything, might even do something to my helicopter to get even.

From most standpoints my rationalization seemed a little irrational, even to me, but I couldn't get rid of the feeling that I was in danger.

While I was looking for another job, my anger began to branch out. Until then almost all of it had been related to work. But when the community center in Kihei put nightlights on their tennis courts, I got unreasonably upset. They were several miles away, but the only bright light between our house and the ocean. More than once I contemplated setting up a mortar and blowing them to pieces.

I was also getting mad at Kathy. It wasn't much, little things like her forgetting to get something at the store, or questioning my judgment on an inconsequential matter. However, the displeasure I expressed belied what I felt. Inside, in my heart, the anger was inexplicably strong. It rose quickly and didn't want to stop.

Getting mad at Kathy for no reason worried me. We'd been together six years and were still best friends. I loved her and had nothing but respect for the way she led her life. Yet small things continued to upset me, and I had no idea why. For her part, Kathy took my criticism in stride, protesting without arguing.

The next job I got was flying for a small tour company in Kahului. Six months after I went to work the owner hit a power line in the Keanae Valley. A passenger died and he injured his back. When I found out he wasn't going to get another helicopter I began looking for my next job.

Unfortunately, that one didn't last much longer than the others. However, it wasn't a problem with either my employer or me. It was my health.

11

The first time it happened was outside Fort Yukon five months before I met Kathy. I was on a weeklong job in the early spring, flying some microwave communications repair guys into the Chandalar Mountains.

One morning I felt sick to my stomach not long after we took off. The nausea passed, but half an hour later I landed on a frozen river, got out of the helicopter and threw up. I didn't feel terribly ill, but I couldn't keep the contents of my stomach down either.

I felt nauseous on and off for the rest of the day, threw up again that night and the next day. All the while I wasn't able to eat. By the third day I was getting pretty weak and felt I shouldn't be flying people around the mountains. Back in Fairbanks, I couldn't remember the name of the last regular doctor I'd seen, so I went to the guy who gave me my annual flight physical.

"Doing poorly," is what he wrote on his examination sheet, and took a blood sample. Later that day he called and said my white blood cell count was very high. "Have you drunk any stream water or been exposed to surface water," he asked. When I said it was possible, he told me I might have giardia, "Beaver Fever," a common intestinal bug from polluted water that makes you very sick. It was common in the spring.

The medicine he prescribed was strong, sickening in itself, but seemed to take care of the problem. Later that summer I got sick again. The flight surgeon treated me for giardia once more. A few weeks later, when it happened a third time, he tried erythromycin, an antibiotic.

That was the last time I threw up for four years. I'd get bouts of nausea after a week or two of flying long days, but they never lasted long. It bothered me, feeling sick for no reason, but I couldn't explain it and usually didn't have the time to dwell on it either. Then, in the middle of our last field season with Forestry Sciences Lab, I got extremely sick.

I had just dropped off the last crew on an island 40 miles west of Juneau when I recognized the queasy feeling. Unlike the nausea in Fort Yukon there was also pain, and it was growing stronger.

Halfway back to the airport I was sure I was going to have to throw up, but I was over water. By the time I reached land I was so sick I had to keep going to Juneau. If I landed to throw up I knew I'd never get in the air again.

Ten minutes later I was at the airport on my hands and knees beside my helicopter, throwing up uncontrollably. During the interminable drive to the hospital I retched every two or three minutes even though my stomach was empty, and the pain was intense. The epicenter was in my lower abdomen, an agonizing ache that grew in blinding waves that doubled me over in agony.

By the time the cab dropped me off at the hospital, my face was covered in cold sweat and I could barely see or think. Everything ached and I was trembling.

At some point I noticed that the pain faded for a second or two after the waves of vomiting peaked. In the beginning I looked forward to the short break, but soon realized that the momentary lapse just let the whole thing begin again. Over and over I got to feel the pain go from almost nothing to its full intensity. It was torture.

At the hospital, when I begged them for something to kill the pain, they asked me if I was a drug addict. Even after I told them what was going on, that it had happened before, they didn't give me a painkiller. Instead, they examined me, drew blood and sent if off to the lab. It seemed like I lay in the emergency room for hours, retching and wondering why they weren't helping me.

Finally the lab report came back. The blood-work up showed an extremely high white blood cell count, indicative of infection, and the nurse gave me some antibiotics and a great big shot of Demerol. As the potent painkiller made its way to my brain everything got better. A peaceful feeling settled over me and I relaxed. I could not remember being in worse pain, or feeling as

---

45

much relief when it was finally over.

Before I left the hospital the next day, the doctor and I talked about the bouts of nausea I'd had over the years. He told me I might have an extremely persistent case of giardia, but the bottom line was, without conducting more tests he couldn't be sure. Since we weren't going to be in Juneau much longer, and I was feeling a lot better, I told him I'd take care of it later.

That fall the flight surgeon in Fairbanks set me up for a bunch of tests. I stuck with it through the barium swallows and enemas, but quit after the sigmoid scope. All they found from that intrusive examination were signs of inflammation from the barium enema they'd given me earlier that week. Once again the flight surgeon wrote a prescription to treat giardia, which I didn't get filled.

I continued to feel nauseous on and off for the next two years, but managed to avoid throwing up until I was at my third helicopter company in Hawaii. The bout was not as bad as the one in Juneau. The pain wasn't nearly as intense; still, it put me in the hospital for a few days.

They ran more tests. My white blood cell count was high again, but they had no idea what the problem was. Neither did I. By that time, however, I was relatively certain flying aggravated the situation. There was a pattern. I was fine until I flew more than three long days in a row. Any time after that, I could get sick in a matter of minutes. But it didn't happen every time, which was frustrating.

I didn't want to go back to the hospital again, so I quit flying until I could figure out what was going on. For a couple of months I was perfectly happy. I missed seeing the island from the air, but was glad not to have to deal with tourists. Similar to the way I felt about my passengers in Alaska, they'd begun to bother me.

The slightest excuse, even their appearance sometimes, could do it. Usually I'd just glare at them, but often I disliked them intensely. It was also nice not to have to worry about getting sick. It wasn't until after I quit flying that I realized how much I dreaded the bouts of incessant puking.

Kathy began looking for work not long after I stopped flying. It didn't take long to cover what was available in her field, and it wasn't encouraging. The few jobs for a wildlife biologist were taken and people were waiting in line. So we both began looking for work outside our professions.

After a month of checking ads, networking with friends and being creative, the only thing we came up with was crewing on a charter fishing boat, which we both did part time for a while. It seemed that all the interesting and profitable jobs available required more education or experience than I had; whereas, Kathy was overqualified.

While I was lamenting the lack of opportunities one day, Kathy said, "Why don't you write a book?"

"What are you talking about?" I asked testily. I was already in a bad mood, and thought she was being flippant while I was trying to address a legitimate concern.

"It's something you once told me you wanted to do. Well, how about now?" she said, ignoring my tone.

Just the fact that it wasn't my idea was enough to disqualify the notion. "I'm trying to come up with something that will make money," I replied curtly.

I knew I'd become defensive and was overreacting to small and insignificant things, but blamed it on the uncertainty in our lives, the frustration I was feeling in everything from my abdominal issues to our financial future. However, I realized it was more than external pressures when I completely lost it with Mo.

Our dog had grown into a handsome hound; all 120 pounds of him, with soft brown eyes set in a bear-sized head. He was a beast, and a really nice dog with only one bad habit. He loved to herd cows.

Most of the year the pastures around our house were full of big brown bovines grazing peacefully on the side of the volcano. I could understand Mo's desire to chase them, the way one good bark could create so much activity, the thrill of controlling the stampede, but I couldn't tolerate his ignoring me when I called him back.

He may not have known how hard it was on the old fat girls and the calves trying to keep up with them, or that chasing them could cause pregnant cows to abort. But Mo did know that when he went after them it made me mad, and apparently he couldn't care less.

47

One afternoon the cows were right up against the fence of our property, mooing and tugging at the grass. I knew it would be hard for Mo to resist chasing them, so I had him lie down not far from where I was working. In a matter of seconds he was gone.

I thought he'd literally disappeared until I saw the tall grass near the fence moving. For a moment I stood in awe. That damned dog was crawling to the cows on his belly. As I dropped my shovel and broke into a run, Mo realized he'd been seen and stepped through the barbed wire fence. The chase was on.

"Mo!" I kept screaming as I ran to the fence and scrambled through.

The big dog swung to the far side of thirty or forty cows, totally ignoring me as he began the round up. It looked as if he was off and running, but I knew his tactics. After Mo got the far side of the herd moving, he'd come back for the cows closer to me.

Sure enough, seconds later he was coming right at me, so close he couldn't ignore me when I yelled as loud as I could. In the brief moment Mo hesitated, I closed the distance between us and grabbed his collar. He twisted and turned, trying to get back to the cows thundering across the pasture, but I was livid and wasn't about to let go.

When we got to the fence I paused. My lower back was in agony from dragging Mo along. There was no way I was going to lift the heavy beast over the three-foot fence. If I couldn't get him over the fence, I reasoned, he'd have to go through. So I wrestled the struggling animal onto his side and held him down with his collar, then crawled between the lower two strands of wire. With a firm grip, I began to pull.

Mo began to fight when he realized what I was up to, twisting and turning, planting his enormous paws when he could. Sweat stung my eyes and I wasn't sure how I was going to get him to my side without the barbwire cutting him, or if I could even get him through the fence at all. He was a big animal.

Then Mo looked at me, let out a frustrated whine, and twisted his head violently to break my grip, bending my wrist back painfully. That's when I lost it and effortlessly pulled him through the fence. I'd never felt anything like that burst of strength, or the intense anger that precipitated it.

We ended up on the ground just inside the wire, lying side-by-side looking at each other. Then Mo lunged at me. I still had his collar clenched in my fist so he didn't get very far, but as we struggled his massive jaws closed on my other hand breaking the skin on three fingers.

When I yelped and almost let go, he went for me again. Instinctively I tightened my grip on his collar, twisting the leather strap around my knuckles. The harder Mo struggled the more I tightened my grip, until his eyes rolled up into his head. He'd run out of oxygen. Immediately I let go of his collar and he regained his senses.

As we lay in the grass staring at each other, I told the dog, "You've got to stop chasing cows, Mo." At the mention of the word "cows", his ears went up and he glanced left and right expectantly.

My irritation at Mo was justifiable, but the anger and disregard for the pain I might have caused our dog wasn't, and I thought I knew why. Staying home, taking care of chores, working on the place was relaxing at first, and a nice vacation in Hawaii. Unfortunately, I'd begun to feel worthless, and believed that my anger at Kathy and Mo was in large part due to my dwindling self-esteem.

I knew that getting a job would help me feel better about life and myself. We also needed the income. Almost everything we'd brought from Alaska, including the money from my house in California, was tied up in our home on the side of a volcano.

I had to find work, no matter what it was. Flying was out, and the only other job that made sense was real estate. Sales on the island were strong and prices high. When we were looking for land I learned quite a bit about the island's real estate market. I also knew how houses were built and their relative costs. The more I thought about it, the more I realized real estate was right for me.

12

After a few weeks of classes and a test, I was having a great time showing people properties for sale, everything from cottages in the jungle to luxury condos along the beach. The job even came with a social life.

Most days I'd have lunch and a drink with other realtors to compare notes on listings and potential clients. However, after a few months and no sales, I was beginning to wonder what was going on. I seemed to be in the wrong place all the time, getting people who were only looking while other agents in the office got the ones who were buying. The problem had to be me, I knew, but couldn't see what it was.

Before long, my inability to make a sale became frustration. If I went into real estate to feel better about myself, it was a mistake. In four months I hadn't made a dime, and it felt like I never would, which was troubling. We were getting low on money, which usually wasn't a big deal. When we had less, we spent less. When we ran out, we went back to work. Unfortunately, real estate was a last chance of sorts.

Our financial situation apparently wasn't bothering Kathy. She'd been looking for work, but was being too selective as far as I was concerned. I knew that the few jobs on the island for wildlife biologists were hard to get, but thought that there were a lot of other things she could be considering.

When I tried to talk to Kathy about the things that were bothering me, it seemed to me that she either had no idea what I was talking about or didn't want to understand. It was frustrating and made me mad.

The anger would subside almost as quickly as it arose, and I always felt justified. Afterwards, however, I frequently saw that I had kept the argument going well beyond the point of reason. I told myself I was just reinforcing a point, but when I tried to exercise some control over my tirades, I couldn't.

The more I got upset, the more often I found myself backed into a corner, and said things that were less than rational, or patently wrong. Even so, I very seldom apologized. Admitting I was wrong would be more evidence of ineptness, which is how it felt, as if I lacked the skills to manage my own life.

Meanwhile, real estate was making me sick, literally. In an effort to get at least one sale, I was driving all over the island, showing everything I could. Like flying, lots of time in the car was upsetting my guts. The nausea usually didn't last long; however, I couldn't get over the fear of the pain and delirium that accompanied the attacks of vomiting. I began to worry.

Driving a lot was having other consequences. I was getting pissed off in traffic. As the density of cars around me increased, I began to feel claustrophobic, then angry. Often I saw hatred in the eyes of drivers in the oncoming lane.

Not long after that, the pressure I felt in traffic became aggression. It began when someone crossed into my lane and I reacted by crossing into his. There was never a threat of collision, but my intent was obvious.

The drink I usually had at lunch had turned into three or four, frequently by myself. I had lost touch with the realtors I'd been getting together with. One afternoon I came home so drunk I couldn't remember where I'd been. There was only the dim recollection of a car driving on the shoulder of the road, horn blaring, to avoid running into me.

The fruitless open house and condo showings had become depressing. In a notebook I kept for work I wrote things like "dumb shits," referring to clients. One of the last things I put down was, "Really starting to hate myself." A number of entries had been thoroughly scratched out, over and over again.

By every standard, I was a failure. I felt isolated, bitter. That's why I was drinking too much, I told myself. My life sucked. So I quit trying to be a realtor.

Things weren't going well with Kathy either. She'd been slowly withdrawing in front of the onslaught of my fault finding and anger. It felt like we were leading separate lives.

As the condition of our lives deteriorated, my anger grew. At some point it reached critical mass and became rage. One minute I would be upset about something, the next I'd be so mad I could barely see. It reminded me of the white phosphorus grenades we used in Vietnam to set things on fire. Once you pulled the pin, the intensely hot reaction was capable of burning through steel underwater, and it didn't stop until it had burned itself out.

The trigger for my rage could be anything, but the reaction was always the same. In a heartbeat I'd be raging at Kathy about some injustice. When she defended herself it felt like an attack, and I'd redouble my efforts. The rants never lasted more than a few minutes, and usually ended with my walking away. Once I was alone it was surprising how quickly the anger dissipated, and how soon I could think clearly again.

Life got even more difficult for Kathy and Mo after I quit real estate and was home all day again. However, there was an upside. In the confined environment of our house, with my outbursts frequent and arguments usually flawed, I could no longer pretend my anger was reasonable. I realized that trying to defend myself was an untenable position. It only made me look stupid. So I began to apologize when I got mad and said rash things.

It wasn't as humiliating as I thought it would be, and before long I found more solace in apologizing than in winning an argument. In conceding the point I effectively took away the source of contention and, in a round about way, won. Well, at least it kept me from being wrong quite as often.

Another benefit, apologizing always took the edge off my anger. Admitting I was wrong, or that it was my fault, was a different kind of control than I was used to. It was passive, quick and easy, and quite often made me look good.

It was right around then that I saw myself stab Kathy in the back.

13

Until I saw myself stab Kathy in the back, my problems seemed to be secondary incidents, situational. Afterwards, I knew how deep the issues were and began to deal with them. Unfortunately, progress was slow.

Kathy was seeing things differently too. She'd been as patient as anyone could be, but my outbursts had taken their toll and she had begun to fight back. I certainly couldn't blame her, considering the frequency and force of my attacks; however, my wife didn't know how screwed up I was.

Because I'd been open, told her about things such as my intrusive thoughts, I assumed Kathy had a good idea of what was going on inside my head. I even thought she knew, without me having to tell her, when I was having a hard time. This wasn't true.

Often I'd mention something relevant to my thoughts or feelings, expecting a sympathetic, or at least heartfelt, response, only to have Kathy stare at me with a blank expression on her face.

I thought the reaction meant she didn't care, that she was intentionally widening the gap between us; while, in reality she had no idea what I was talking about. So, it was good for both of us when Kathy finally asked me what was wrong.

She'd just gotten home from town. I'd been having another bad day, a costly mistake on the house, and then I got mad at Mo for something. But I was aware of my disposition and consciously made an effort not to let it show.

"How'd the shopping go?" I asked.

"The usual," she responded.

There was the familiar flat tone in her voice, as if she were answering questions in a police lineup. Kathy was already leery, and all I'd done was ask a simple question.

"How's your day been?" she asked, holding me with a steady gaze.

"Not that good," I admitted looking down. Avoiding her eyes made it easier for me to focus. "Had some problems with the drywall. Then Mo…"

"He wouldn't come out of his doghouse when I got home," she interjected.

When I looked up she was glaring at me. I knew what she was doing, changing the subject. "The god damned dog," I began, feeling my chest tighten and the anger begin to rise. "I turn my back on him for a second…"

"You don't have to yell," she interrupted calmly.

She's changing the subject again, I thought, turning it on me, making it my fault. "I'm not yelling!" I told her.

I knew I was talking louder than usual, could feel the force behind my words, the tension in my muscles, the aggression, but I hadn't started it, goddamn it. I was actually trying hard not to lose my temper. With that thought in mind, I watched her, waiting. There was no going back, only walking away, and I wasn't angry enough yet.

Kathy usually found something else to do when I said something as stupid as "I'm not yelling," when I obviously was. Instead she stared back.

"What's going on, Tom?" she asked patiently. "You can't go around taking it out on the defenseless…"

The anger surged, on the brink of rage. Then, just as quickly dropped to almost nothing. As my head cleared I heard Kathy asking, "And why are you…?"

"I'm sorry, Kat," I cut her off. I already knew what she was going to say, and listening to what felt like a lecture was only going to piss me off again. "I don't know what's going on. I really don't. I know it's not his fault, or yours."

She visibly relaxed, and asked, "Okay, but why the anger? The way you look at me sometimes, the tone in your voice… it's like you hate me."

"I don't hate you," I stated emphatically, feeling the weight of those words, knowing I had to go further. "I know what you're seeing. It's unbridled anger. It looks like hatred. It even feels like hatred to me sometimes. But it isn't. I swear, it isn't." I wanted her to feel as certain as I did, that what I felt wasn't hatred for her.

Kathy's expression softened. "Well, that's nice to know," she said.

I could have left it at that, but didn't want to stop. "When I get upset I feel it here," I told her, placing a hand on my chest. "It really doesn't matter what you say or do. The anger's there just waiting for something to let it loose. You'll say something, do something, and I feel it start to grow. Then something else happens and I get madder. It builds on itself. There's pressure in my head by then and it starts screwing up my thoughts, turning things around. I start bringing in anything I can to support what I'm thinking, shit from the past, making conjectures. It gets ridiculous, but I can't stop my mind from going there." I felt I should go on, but wasn't sure where. "It's not hatred. Or you, or Mo. I know it's not right, but..."

When I paused to collect my thoughts, Kathy asked, "If you're that aware of it, and know it's wrong, why don't you do something about it?"

"You'd think I could," I agreed. "But the rational part of my mind disappears. Actually, more like it's pushed out of the picture. It's as if a separate mentality takes over and it's already pissed off and wants to get madder. That's what you're seeing. Not hatred for you."

Kathy looked at me for a while. "That's reassuring," she said with a smile. "But sounds a little wacko."

She was right. It was crazy and she obviously had no idea how bad it was. I decided it was time to change that.

"It gets worse," I told her. "There's a point when it becomes rage. A flashpoint where that anger goes from my chest right into my brain. The pressure inside my head is so strong I can feel it pushing against my skull. That's what you see when I'm ranting and raving."

"Is the... the rage there because you're angry at me?" Kathy asked cautiously.

I nodded. "Yes, but it goes way beyond you. The threat is larger, everywhere, overwhelming. My anger's directed at you because I feel like I'm under attack. And you're the only living thing around."

"You think I'm attacking you?" she asked.

"Yes. Mercilessly, and I have to defend myself. Nothing else matters. That's what it feels like."

Kathy thought a few seconds, then asked, "This attacking... I mean, the rage, irrational thinking, it's not like..."

I knew where she was going. Around that time "going postal" was synonymous with Vietnam veterans. "No," I laughed mirthlessly. "You mean like a flashback where I flip out and shoot you. I don't get those. Anyway, it's not that kind of thing. When I feel under attack it's more like being in the middle of a storm than a war. It's disorienting, confusing, and behind it all is this immense pressure. I know I'm losing control, which of course is frustrating and adds to the anger." I certainly could have ended it there, but if Kathy was willing to listen there was something else I wanted her to know. "Want to hear more?" I asked.

"Sure," she replied.

"I really have been working on this anger thing. You know, trying to figure out what's happening and, like you said, get control of it," I told her then paused. I knew what I wanted to say, but wasn't sure it was going to make sense. "At one point I took on the rage, actually tried to keep it from making it to my brain."

I told Kathy about the technique I'd learned from the lawyer in California after Darcie walked out on me, the one where I visualized the tape recorder and pushed the "off" button.

"Well, I modified that technique," I continued. "Instead of seeing the button and pushing it, I visualized my hands reaching inside my chest and wrapping themselves around the surging anger, choking it off as it rushed to my head." I laughed cynically, remembering the incident vividly. "For a second I thought it was working. Actually, a little less than a second, before it shot through my hands like..."

"You could actually see it?" Kathy asked, incredulously.

"Yeah," I replied sincerely. "It turned into a shard of steel, a shinny tapered spike that shot straight into my brain." She didn't say anything, just looked at me. "I know it sounds weird, Kat, but that's what I saw."

"That is weird," she agreed, and then added, "I think it's definitely time for you to see someone. Get professional help." After a pause, she added, "I don't think you're crazy. But you can't let this become your life."

I didn't tell my wife that it already was my life, but for a change I took her suggestion positively. "That's not a bad idea," I agreed. "Unfortunately, it'll have to wait a while. We don't have health insurance."

Talking to Kathy about my anger issues helped as much as telling her about my intrusive thoughts. Inside my mind the anger was suppressed, waiting around to be provoked. Outside my head it had a name, became more tangible, could be dealt with on a different level.

Talking to Kathy about it appeared to be good for her too. She seemed to navigate my mood swings more effectively, weather my tirades or disregard them entirely. She didn't take it personally anymore.

Other than the poor state of our finances, for all intents and purposes, life seemed to be good again. However, I was beginning to see the good times for what they were, plateaus. Sometimes they lasted for days, but more often it was a matter of hours. Regardless, I appreciated every minute because on those plateaus I was myself; the person I'd been and wanted to be, a person who felt good about himself and his life.

14

For quite awhile Kathy had been telling me my breath was not pleasant. At first it was only now and then, so I wrote it off to bad hygiene. When she began to bring it up more often I took offense. I couldn't smell anything. However, after she began to pull away in revulsion almost every time we got close, I decided to have it checked out.

There was a Veterans Administration outpatient clinic on Maui, so I made an appointment to see them. The Army doctors put my jaw back together after I was shot down, but the VA took care of the follow up work. They paid for a civilian dentist to put a bridge in place of my teeth that were knocked out. They also took care of an impacted molar ten years later. I was hoping they could help me with the bad breath problem.

The people at the VA clinic were as nice as they could be, and made an appointment for me with a local dentist. It took him about a minute to decide that I should see an oral surgeon.

Two days later I was in the surgeon's office and he told me that the root of a tooth was seriously infected. The whole thing had to come out. He went on to explain that the impact that broke my jaw also drove the tooth through a membrane that separates teeth from bone, and infection had set in. He took it out, and a week later a bridge was being made to replace it.

The VA handled my dental issues so quickly, and with such efficiency, I couldn't help but wonder if they could do the same for my abdominal issues. Maybe they would be able to tell me why I threw up uncontrollably.

A few weeks later the VA flew me to its hospital on Oahu where a gastroenterologist listened to my accounts of vomiting, pain and hospital visits. He came up with the usual, giardia or irritable bowel syndrome, and suggested I follow up with a doctor closer to home. He said the VA would pay for the consultations.

With not much else to do I began making the rounds on Maui, visiting every doctor on the island that knew anything about internal medicine, but none of them had any new ideas. The consensus was irritable bowel syndrome, but that would only explain the queasy feelings and not the violent vomiting, much less the intense pain.

Finally, I ran into Reginald Buesa, a Filipino doctor who'd just gotten out of medical school. "So you think it happens when you spend too much time in the helicopter," he surmised after I told him about the connection between flying long days and the onset of throwing up.

"Yes," I replied.

"And that involves lots of sitting, correct?" he asked.

"That's right," I told him.

"And you say that the army doctors preformed a laparotomy?"

I pulled up the front of my Aloha shirt and showed him the eight-inch scar that began below my ribs and ran around my bellybutton.

The young doctor looked at me for a few seconds, then, almost as an aside, he mentioned, "It could be adhesions."

"What?" I asked. I'd never heard of them.

"Intestinal adhesions," he said almost reluctantly. When I shrugged he went on. "Mostly women get them. After C-sections, things like that, but men can have them too."

"Okay," I responded. "Why do you think I'd have them?"

The doctor pointed to my stomach. "The laparotomy. You say they did that in the Army. When they cut you open after your accident." He seemed uncomfortable again. "It's just one of any number of things that might be the cause of your problems."

I was amazed. How many had there been? At least half a dozen doctors had examined me since I began having problems with my guts. If I hadn't told them about the surgery they must have seen the scar on my stomach during their examinations.

I could feel the anger rising. "What are they?" I asked.

"Well, let me see." He paused. "Tissue, scar tissue in this case, that binds the intestines to each other. Most likely secondary

59

to the operation in the Army."

"But, would that make me throw up? Could it cause the pain?"

"Absolutely," the doctor told me. "The adhesions cause the intestine to twist. For instance, if you have a garden hose and twist it, what happens?" he inquired.

"Stops flowing," I said.

"That's right, same in the intestines," he said, obviously pleased with my comprehension. "Food, everything stops flowing and you get very, very sick," he added, making an appropriately serious Yuk face.

A mechanical obstruction in my guts made perfectly good sense. But if it was as simple as that, why hadn't at least one of the other doctors looked into the possibility of... "What are they called?" I had to ask again.

"Adhesions," he told me patiently.

"How come none of the other doctors I've seen mentioned adhesions?" I asked.

He looked extremely uncomfortable at that point, and avoided eye contact. For a moment I thought the doctor wasn't going to answer, but finally. "Maybe nobody told you because it's very hard to diagnose. Adhesions don't appear on X-rays... soft tissue. Short of an exploratory operation, there's no way to be certain that's the problem."

"I see," I replied, finally understanding his moments of discomfort. It was a liability issue. "I really appreciate your telling me this, doctor. Thank you very much."

Dr. Buesa had another appointment so I left with some serious questions, like how dangerous are they, how do I get rid of them? I didn't feel like waiting for answers so I went to the library at Maui Memorial Hospital. Several hours later I had a good idea of what was going on.

The intestines, suspended inside the abdominal cavity, are in constant motion. Any outside influence, disease, surgery, or even severe bruising, can create scar tissue that forms a hard spot in the otherwise soft pliable tissue. As the intestines move they can kink and knot around the hard spot, blocking the flow of bacterium-laden body waste, allowing it to leach into the body through the walls of the intestine.

That's where the nausea and pain came from, as I understood it. Antibiotics and other drugs weren't very effective against blockage because of the intestines' one-way absorption process.

If left untreated, obstructed bowels decay. Toxins move quickly through the abdominal cavity, blood and lymph systems. In worse case scenarios death can come in a matter of hours. The only remedy I found in my brief research was surgery.

The next day I was back in Dr. Buesa's office. "So, what do you think I should do?" I asked, after telling him what I'd read.

"This is up to you," he said.

"What do you mean?"

"It depends on how sick you are," he told me. "If you are not very sick, it is best to live with it. If you are very sick you may want to have surgery."

"Well, I get very sick," I reasoned. "But not that often."

"You should know there is always a risk of creating more adhesions by undergoing surgery," he cautioned. That was something else I'd read in the hospital library. Men, while less likely to get adhesions than women, are prone to reoccurrence after surgery.

"I understand," I responded, having decided to live with it.

Adhesions could be deadly, but they could also be taken care of by a surgeon in a matter of minutes. So, I did my best not to think about them, or surgery; however, anytime I felt nauseous or something moved in my guts, I had to wonder if I might be heading to the hospital soon.

Knowing what ailed me had drawbacks, like knowing adhesions could kill me, but overall it was better than having no idea of what was going on. There wasn't much I could do, but at least I was in position to make decisions, take a little control, something that was sorely missing in my life.

Even though nothing had really changed, I felt better. I even thought my temper wasn't quite as bad, until I mentioned it to Kathy.

"According to whom?" she asked with a laugh.

Not long after Dr. Buesa diagnosed my adhesions I got a letter from the Veterans Administration. It concerned the tooth removed by the oral surgeon. The letter said the VA was satisfied with the work and was glad to have been of service. In conclusion the letter stated, that if I ever needed any more work done on teeth "12 & 25," they would take care of it. I read the last part again. The letter implied only those two teeth were covered by the VA.

I wasn't sure where tooth 12 and tooth 25 were, but I knew that more than two of my teeth had been damaged when I was shot down. A few were knocked out in the crash and several more removed in the field hospital because they were broken.

When I called the dental department at the VA's regional office in Honolulu to see if there was some kind of mistake, I was told, no. The person on the phone was certain my records showed only teeth 12 and 25 had been damaged. When I asked him to mail a copy of the records, I was given an address in St. Louis.

I was surprised how blunt the person had been, and perturbed that the VA could make a mistake like that. Regardless, I did the only thing I could, wrote a letter to St. Louis requesting copies of my records.

Life was getting grim again. Nothing had really been resolved with my abdominal issues. Most likely the problem was intestinal adhesions, but without an operation there was no way to know. Even with surgery, there was no certain cure. And, if my anger had been on a break, it had come roaring back.

I was getting pissed off at everything, and still had no idea why I was having homicidal thoughts about my wife. Added to all of that was the whole thing with teeth 12 and 25. Also, the cash we got for selling our car and truck was getting low. To pay bills, we had sold the new truck and car we'd brought to Hawaii when we moved from Alaska, and replaced them with a well used Subaru.

Understandably, I was about as down as I thought I could be, until we found out the pasture we lived in was being subdivided. Then I fell off a cliff. The land that surrounded us belonged to the Department of Hawaiian Homelands: a state agency in charge of managing and ceding state land back to native Hawaiians.

The agency had been around for a long time and was notorious for moving incredibly slowly on just about everything. People were dying while they waited for their land.

Nothing changed until the issue got national media coverage. According to what I read, Congress told Hawaiian

Homelands that they had to do something or the federal government would take over. I believed that ceding the land to its rightful owners was legally and morally correct, right up to the day we heard they were going to develop the pastures around us.

"They won't be able to do it," I declared.

"Why not?" Kathy asked.

"Hawaiian Homelands is broke," I explained. "They can't build here because we're out in the country. The infrastructure, roads and utilities, would bankrupt them. Besides, there aren't any jobs up here, not even a store to buy food within half an hour."

A couple of months later, we learned that Hawaiian Home Lands was putting its subdivision right down our driveway, a home site every couple of hundred feet, and absolutely no improvements. There'd be no electricity, water or sewer. It would be a mess. With the added traffic my half-mile rutted dirt road would become impassable every time it rained.

In an instant, everything we'd done in the last few years seemed pointless. I went ballistic. The reason we had bought land in the middle of a pasture was for privacy, for the luxury of being by ourselves. That would soon be gone. I felt sick. It was time to move, I decided. Leave my failed plans behind. Then the financial repercussions dawned on me.

We were looking at losing tens of thousands of dollars. The greatest value of our home was its location, the beautiful views and tranquility. With a subdivision moving in, half of that value was gone.

Nevertheless, we figured it was better to sell, take a loss, and make new plans.

- 15 -

Life was out of control again. I knew from experience what a downhill slide looked like, and I was in a bad one. For quite a while I'd been thinking about talking to a psychiatrist about my intrusive thoughts and anger issues. Kathy had suggested it several times. So, I figured it was as good a time as any to see if psychiatric counseling could help. We still didn't have insurance, but when I was at the VA hospital in Honolulu I walked right by their psychiatric clinic.

After waiting several weeks for an appointment, they flew me to Oahu where I gave the VA psychiatrist a brief history of my life. After I told him about my last helicopter crash, intrusive thoughts, anger, back problems, uncontrollable vomiting, and employment issues, he asked some routine questions, such as, was I sleeping well, and did I have flashbacks? I told him I slept fine but had nightmares. The doctor didn't even ask what they were about, so I didn't bother to tell him about the night sweats.

I thought the trip to Oahu had been a waste of time until a letter arrived from the VA saying they had approved outpatient services for a mental health provider of my choice on Maui. The news made me happier than I'd expected, and my confidence in the VA rose.

The next thing to do was find a competent doctor, one who knew something about veterans' issues. It made sense to ask other veterans, so I went to the next meeting of the Vietnam Veterans of Maui.

It was a small group, twenty or thirty people, but dynamic. Members ranged from neat businessmen to nasty looking guys in camouflage fatigues. They talked about projects underway to raise money for the group, comrades that weren't doing well, and the

64

state of veterans' affairs in general.

Before too long I began to feel uncomfortable, a little claustrophobic. All the talk about veterans and their problems was too much. What they were doing was good, but I just didn't want to be involved, or even listen to it for that matter, so I left.

Outside the door there was a big guy smoking a cigarette. I asked him if he knew of any psychiatrists who worked with vets. "There's this guy, Rick Sword," he told me. "Over in Kahului. He's great."

A few days later I was in Rick's office. He was a psychologist, not a psychiatrist. I wasn't exactly sure what the difference was, but Rick didn't look like any kind of doctor. He met me at the door with a big handshake, and "Hey! How you doin', man." Everything from the radiant aloha shirt to his broad smile was too cheerful to be taken seriously.

After some small talk Rick had me fill out paperwork for the VA and take a bunch of multiple choice tests related to stress and social functions. Then, in what was becoming a routine, I told him about my problems and me.

When I came back the next week the tests were scored. "I think PTSD is playing a major role in your life," he told me after another big handshake.

I'd been hearing about PTSD since the late seventies, and gone through a spectrum of thoughts and feelings on the subject over the last seven or eight years, vacillating between empathy and condemnation.

Essentially, I didn't know much about it. Recently though, I'd read that there were a lot more guys out there with Post Traumatic Stress Disorder than the army was admitting, that only a fraction of a percent were hurting anyone but themselves, and that they were suffering without help.

At that point I decided that PTSD was real. However, other than the fact we'd fought a war together, which was no small deal, I couldn't see any connections between the veterans I was hearing about and me.

"I'm not sure that's it," I responded. He was moving way too fast. I hadn't even convinced myself being in his office was the right thing to do. How was I supposed to believe his snap judgment?

65

"Why not?" he returned.

"For one thing," I explained patiently. "I'm not really sure what PTSD is. But if it's what I think it is, a problem with what I did in the war, I'm pretty sure that's not what's happening. It just doesn't relate." Rick just looked at me when I finished.

"What I did in Vietnam doesn't bother me." I continued. "I wasn't blowing up babies. I was fighting regular soldiers, NVA, guys who'd come down from North Vietnam to take over the country. I did my job and came home. For another thing, it's been fifteen years. If I was going to have problems with what I did then, they'd have surfaced by now."

"Let me ask you a question," Rick said, leaning back in his chair. "What kind of kid were you. You know, before you went into the Army?"

"I don't know," I replied. "Fairly normal. I got in trouble a lot, but nothing very bad."

"Did you want to kill people?"

"Of course not," I replied, instantly annoyed.

"And after you got back from the Nam?"

I never liked it when people called Vietnam, "the Nam," even if they'd been there. But I didn't let it distract me. I wanted to work with this guy, and it didn't take much thought to see where he was going with that question. "Okay," I admitted. "I hung out by myself in the mountains, drank a lot, slept with a loaded gun by my bed. Normal stuff like that."

Rick laughed, and asked, "Then what?"

He knew the answer, but I went through it anyway. "Tried college, again," I told him. "Couldn't stay in. Traveled a lot for a few years. Never stayed anywhere more than a couple months. Then I met Darcie and ended up in Alaska."

"You see the pattern, don't you?" Rick asked.

"What do you mean? That I moved around a lot?"

Rick ignored me. "You told me it's been fifteen years, that it should have surfaced by now. Right?" He was grinning. "Well, guess what. It did. You came back and self-medicated yourself with anything you could find. When that didn't work you took off, and have been running away from your problems ever since."

"Bullshit," I told him. "First of all, I like to go out and drink. You can call it self-medication, but it's also a major part of

66

my social life. Secondly, being a helicopter pilot, travel is the nature of my work. And, as far as not being able to stay in one place, how about Alaska?"

"How about Alaska?" he returned, with a big guffaw. "What were you doing up there?"

"Flying," I said.

"What else?"

"Having a good time with Kathy and some friends."

"Yeah," Rick proclaimed. "You stayed in Alaska because flying and Kathy were the perfect combination for you, distraction and security. What more could you ask for... or any of us for that matter?" He laughed again. "Living on the edge, hanging it out everyday in your helicopter. It sure kept you away from what was bugging you. Not to mention a great release for stress and anxiety. When you moved to Hawaii your life slowed down. It almost came to a stop for Christ's sake. And guess what? You're having all kinds of problems."

That actually made a lot of sense. Alaska had been pretty wild. And my life had changed incredibly fast since we'd moved to Hawaii. There was also no denying that Kathy was a good influence. I hadn't thought about her making my life more secure, but it was probably true.

"So you think PTSD is ruining my life?" I asked, going back to what he'd said earlier.

"Not necessarily, but it's sure having an influence."

"So, what is PTSD?" I asked cautiously.

"Next time," he told me.

At the next session we talked about PTSD for a while. Whatever he told me, I forgot before the end of the session. It just didn't make sense. We also talked about my temper.

I mentioned it during the previous session, but had avoided telling him how much of the day I spent in a cesspool of hatred, or how mad I got at Kathy for no reason. It was a picture of myself I didn't like to see, much less show to anyone else.

"Anger," Rick said, when I finally told him how bad it was. "Is completely natural."

"I don't think it's normal," I told him. "Especially when it turns to rage."

"Natural, is what I said," Rick chided. "Not normal. And

what I was going to say before you interrupted is, anger's a natural response to a threat. It helps you focus, adds strength and determination. Makes you a mean mother. As you know, man, it's a pretty common tool in war." The psychologist paused then asked, "Do you drop at loud noises, take cover if a car backfires?"

"Sure," I replied. "But who wouldn't after getting shot at for a year?"

"Okay," Rick responded enthusiastically. "That's a heightened startle reflex, even more common than anger in combat. Just like a startle reflex, guys bring their anger home."

That made sense, in a textbook kind of way. But I wasn't responding to a threat. Other than the report of a rifle or a backfiring car now and then, there weren't any threats. But, before I could go any farther with the thought, Rick asked, "You been having panic attacks?"

"No." I didn't know what they were, but I knew I didn't panic.

"You ever get into denial about things?" he grinned.

"No." I knew what denial was, and I didn't have any reason to use it.

"Look," Rick said confidentially. "Denial isn't as bad as it's cracked up to be. Helps keep things you don't like at the proper distance, makes them easier to deal with. It's only a problem when it goes on too long." Rick watched me for a moment, but when I didn't react, he continued. "So, you're not in denial and you don't get panic attacks. Ever get the feeling that you got to get out of someplace? Like you're trapped?" Rick stopped and looked at me again. "How about . . ."

"I have nightmares," I interrupted, and told him about being in the back of the helicopter that's about to crash.

"Recurring?" he asked.

"Yeah, and sometimes I sweat so much in my sleep it wakes Kathy up. But it doesn't happen a lot."

"And you don't think you're in denial about anything here?" he asked, a look of amazement on his face.

"I'm talking about it, aren't I?" It was a statement, not a question.

"Yeah," Rick responded. "But you are not hearing what you're saying."

The next session we talked about my intrusive thoughts.

"If I had to guess, I'd say it's OCD, Obsessive Compulsive Disorder," Rick told me. "They're not sure exactly what causes it. Clinically. But it's an anxiety related problem. Unwanted thoughts, just like you described, obsessions you don't want but can't stop. Some people think it's actually a way to reduce anxiety. The whole obsessive compulsive thing."

I certainly didn't want to be labeled with anything that sounded like Obsessive Compulsive Disorder, and responded with, "I thought obsessing was more like someone washing their hands all the time."

"It can be," my psychologist replied, grinning. "If you're afraid of germs."

"So... I think about a violent act because I'm afraid of violence?" I tried.

"Possibly. But you could think about it just because the thought bothers you."

I was getting confused. "I see," I said.

THE VETERANS ADMINISTRATION

I was in limbo, or possibly purgatory, while we waited for things like our house to sell and my military records to arrive from St. Louis; nothing was happening. Life had come to a standstill of sorts, but it wasn't a break. I still felt the pressure of my problems.

My mind kept turning thoughts over and over, making things as complicated as possible. I worried a lot and that made me irritable. The only relief I got from my agitated state was immersing myself in chores and projects around the house. I also enjoyed the run Kathy and I took most mornings.

One clear blue day we came to the end of Thompson Road, the turnaround point for the run from our house. It dead-ended at a gate that led into the green expanse of Ulupalakua Ranch, one of the most beautiful spots in Hawaii, more than twenty-five thousand acres that stretched from the sea to six thousand feet.

The ranch had a beach, its own lava flows and cinder cones, and pastures that made you want to be a cow. There were also incredible views of the beautiful blue Pacific, the islands of Lani, Molokai, Molokini, and the West Maui Mountains.

As we gazed across the lush pastures of Ulupalakua, watching the cattle graze, Kathy said wistfully, "I wonder if they could use a wildlife biologist?"

"Only one way to find out," I replied.

Pardee Erdman, the owner of Ulupalakua Ranch, hired Kathy at her interview. Along with a decent paycheck, the ranch provided 14 gallons of gas and 10 pounds of beef every other week, and housing. It was like a wave of good fortune washing over us.

A few weeks later we got an offer on our house, which I accepted right away. For the place I thought would be our home forever and had put so much work into, I was amazed how happy I was to leave. Even moving was fun.

While Kathy went to work, I stayed busy fixing up the little ranch house Pardee let us live in. It needed painting, the yard was completely overgrown and there were the daily chores, dishes and shopping, to get done.

It wasn't a particularly glamorous job but I enjoyed the routine and getting things done. Except toilets, I don't do toilets. However, what really made me feel good was the lack of responsibility. No money worries, no house hassles... I just got up everyday, did some chores and went outside to work on a project. There was nothing to worry about.

Pardee hired Kathy because she was a wildlife biologist and he wanted to establish a captive herd of elk in the upper pastures. He was interested in diversifying his cattle and sheep operations by capitalizing on the growing market for game animals among the Pacific Rim countries. With a herd of elk in the Hawaiian Islands, the ranch would be a central location for live sales of the animals to game farms in the Pacific region.

Kathy was the perfect person for the job. Her Master's thesis was on deer. It was also a plus that she'd worked for the government because the first phase of her job was procuring the permits to import elk, and that wasn't going to be easy. Hawaii had been so overrun by introduced plants, animals and diseases that even dogs and cats had to be quarantined for months when their owners brought them to the islands.

She was also going to have to enclose several hundred acres with escape proof game fencing, build a handling facility, locate 50 disease-free, pure-blooded Rocky Mountain elk without the benefit of DNA testing, and transport them to Maui. It was a very interesting and involved project.

While Kathy was working on the permits to bring elk to Hawaii, I finished putting the house and yard in order, and was getting pretty good at shopping. I had all the prices down and knew just where to go for what. I also started a garden and found that working with my hands in the soil was an absorbing pastime. Helping things grow was involved and rewarding, and I got more produce than I expected.

I envied the excitement of Kathy's job, and felt a little bad about her being the only one bringing in money; however, since we'd move to the ranch it had been near impossible not to enjoy my life. If I wasn't working around the house or shopping, I was at the beach riding my boogie board or lying in the sun. I also spent quite a bit of time on the dry, sparsely populated south side of the island. It was mostly broken lava flows with patches of wispy dry grass, strong winds and heavy seas crashing on ragged sea cliffs. I loved the solitude, and often spent entire days there by myself.

With life so good my anger wasn't surfacing as often; however, surprisingly my intrusive thoughts were still coming on strong. And my adhesions were beginning to worry me again. The low-grade nausea that came on after a long day in the cockpit or car was cropping up without provocation. It never got to the point of throwing up, but the change was noticeable and I found myself weighing the pros and cons of surgery, on a daily basis.

When I got back from the beach one day there was a fat brown envelope from St. Louis waiting for me on the kitchen counter. "How long has it been?" Kathy asked, picking it up and handing it to me. "A couple of months?"

"At least," I told her as I tore it open, hoping the package would contain the information I needed to convince the Veterans Administration that more than tooth 12 and 25 were injured when I was shot down.

The records seemed to be complete. There were doctors' notes and reports from the nurses in the ward beginning the moment I arrived at the field hospital. The first thing of interest I came upon was the description of my back injuries:

> There are chip fractures of the anterior superior aspects of the 1st, 2nd and 3rd lumbar vertebrae with minimal compression of the anterior portions of all 3 vertebrae . . .

"Chip fractures" didn't sound good, but my injuries seemed a lot worse at the time. More than once in the past I'd had reason to remember the doctor in the evacuation hospital telling me I might be paralyzed from the waist down.

I really did consider myself lucky to get as much use out of my back as I did. Since we'd moved to the ranch, where I hadn't been asking much of it, my back problems had all but disappeared. About the only issue I still had with it was rolling over and moving around relentlessly at night to get comfortable.

A few pages later I read another doctor's report:

There is a fracture of the condylar neck bilaterally with medial displacement of both condylar neck and head fragments. There is also a comminuted fracture of the anterior portion of the rt. Ramus of the mandible with the fracture fragments held in good position and aligned by wires.

Initially I thought the report was about my neck, but soon realized it was describing the injuries to my jaw. For the first time in more than a dozen years I remembered that day in vivid detail. How I woke up lying on a stretcher in the hallway of a MASH hospital in Tay Ninh, the steady flow of blood in my mouth choking me.

When they put me in traction they strapped me down face up, and the blood from my shattered jaw had no place to go. To keep from choking I kept spitting the coagulating globs into the air, where most of them fell back on my face. All the while someone kept asking me inane questions, like, "What's your mother's name. Where are you from?"

As I recalled the aftermath of the crash, more of the day came into focus, the pain and confusion, and the knowledge that it was entirely my fault.

I'd been flying scouts for nearly a year. The majority of scout pilots didn't make it a month, not including the dropouts. I should have known better than to be in the middle of that field, flying thirty miles an hour, no more than ten feet above the tall grass and brush, surrounded by at least a platoon of guys with machine guns who wanted to kill us.

There was no excusing the mistake, but there were several reasons for it. Several hours earlier we'd flown around the field and determined no one was there. Also, I'd just returned from two weeks of anything but rest and relaxation in Australia. The first day back I logged twelve hours on the Hobbs meter, which translates into fourteen or more hours in the cockpit. The next day

---

74

I was up at dawn. That day Ken Gardiner, my door gunner, and I got shot down. Basically, I was out of shape and exhausted.

The memories kept coming. I could hear the odd sound the bullets made as they went through my helicopter. As if someone was tapping the side with a hammer.

I never got use to being shot at, much less having the aircraft hit. It was like being stung by a bee. All I wanted to do was get the hell out of there; but we were going slowly, and were too far away from the safety of the tree line and cover of the jungle.

Ken's machinegun was hammering away, but it didn't seem to be firing as fast as usual. Everything was taking too long. I looked behind us. North Vietnamese soldiers were standing up, AK 47's kicking in their hands. I turned back to the trees in front of us where we had to be if we wanted to live. We were getting closer.

More bullets hit. I could feel things peppering my face, pieces of metal and Plexiglas dislodged by the 7.62-millimeter rounds. With incredible clarity I could hear the engine coming apart, the sharp "ping" of turbine blades breaking loose at 52,000 rpm and tearing through the engine case and sides of the aircraft. It's a very distinct sound, as was the "engine out" warning horn blaring in my headset.

There was also the unforgettable noise of heavy gears grinding. I'd never heard the sound before that day, but it didn't take long for me to realize that the main transmission had been hit and was on its way to seizing.

At that point I could no longer differentiate between the sounds of combat and my dying helicopter. A quick glance at my instruments showed everything in the red. We weren't going to be flying much longer but we were almost to the edge of the clearing, the safety of the jungle, and we couldn't stay where we were.

The brief relief I felt as we cleared the tree line and the sound of automatic weapons stopped was bittersweet in my memory. Seconds later we settled into the thick canopy of the jungle below us.

The stricken helicopter jerked violently from side to side when the blades hit the trees. Then, for a moment, there was silence. The engine was out and the transmission had stopped turning. I could distinctly hear leaves dragging across the fuselage

---

and limbs snapping as we fell to the jungle floor more than a hundred feet below. I could even remember the last thing I saw, a large tree limb coming up at me.

There were flashes of other memories: regaining consciousness in the mangled cockpit, smelling smoke, waking up again on the ground outside the helicopter, and discovering large ants wallowing in my blood, but one memory made me pause.

There was blood in my mouth, lots of it, and when I spit it out my jaw moved awkwardly, like it was slipping. One side was closing more quickly than the other, and there was a grating sensation. With a vague feeling of revulsion, I knew that what I felt was the ragged edges of bones rubbing together. My jaw was shattered.

I remembered feeling sick and confused, and seeing the crushed helicopter at the foot of an enormous tree about 50 feet from where I lay. A column of pale smoke rose above it and Ken was still in the wreckage. He was slumped over in his seat against the bulkhead in front of him.

I didn't know if he was dead or alive, but couldn't leave him in the helicopter with smoke coming out of the engine compartment. We all feared burning to death.

When I tried to move my body, turn and head towards the helicopter, a flash of pain literally knocked me out. Knowing my back was injured, I moved more cautiously the next time and got a few feet before I pinched something and blacked out again. When I finally got to the crumpled aircraft and Ken, I could see a small stream of blood running out of his mouth, and one of his eyes was hanging out of its socket. It took a few tries to get his seat belt off and pull him out, but when he was on the ground beside me I could tell he was alive.

I was so caught up in the memories of that day, their clarity, letting go was almost a struggle, but a few pages later I found what I was looking for, a reference to my teeth by a doctor at the evacuation hospital in Long Binh. In a comment box he'd written, "trauma to teeth 12 – 25." Evidently, the VA had interpreted the "-" to mean "&." Obviously an oversight, I reasoned.

17

After looking at the records from St. Louis, and recalling what I went through the last time I was shot down, I had two thoughts. First, I was lucky to be alive. Second, if I had dental problems of any kind, the Veterans Administration should be responsible for taking care of them.

So I sent the dental clinic at the Veterans Administration a copy of the report from Vietnam, showing teeth 12 – 25 were injured, along with a brief account of the crash and a letter asking them to set the record straight.

After a few weeks, and no response from the VA, I called the clinic to find out what was going on. I was told there was nothing they could do, that if I wanted to change the rating on my teeth I'd have to open a claim, a written request, to the Veterans Administration.

I was truly disappointed. The VA had always been so agreeable. Now they were turning something simple into a problem, and for no apparent reason. Could be the wrong person, place or time, I thought. The VA is enormous. They're bound to be a little impersonal and make mistakes. But that bothered me just as much. They should care, and shouldn't make mistakes, especially when it involved combat injuries.

When President Lincoln formed the Veterans Administration, he pledged, "To care for him who shall have borne the battle, for his widow and orphan." I read that in a VA brochure. They were there because people got wounded fighting their country's battles and deserved to have their injuries taken care of. My jaw was broken, my teeth damaged, and I felt they should fix them. What was so hard to understand about that?

When I told Rick about the VA's attitude towards my teeth,

he told me that they were right. I should open a claim. He said I was going to have to open one sooner or later if I wanted to keep seeing him. Apparently the VA picked up the bill for a certain amount of care and then you had to go through the claims process, which seemed reasonable.

A few days later I opened a claim with the Veterans Administration's regional office in Honolulu on the neighboring island of Oahu for a review of the dental records from Vietnam and the conditions caused by my broken jaw, and continuing help from Rick. In the claim, I also wrote that I had to quit flying because of adhesions caused by the surgery in Vietnam, and that it was probably going to take another operation to get rid of them.

I hadn't made up my mind to go ahead with it, but had decided that, if I got sick enough to be hospitalized again, that would be a good time to have the adhesions removed. Seeing that the VA often took months to respond to a letter, I thought it prudent to let them know in advance that an operation was imminent and I didn't have the money for it.

The next week I got a reply. "This is just to let you know that we have received your application for benefits. There is no need for you to take any additional action at this time." I relaxed a little. The process had begun. Once they took a look at the facts I believed they'd change their mind about teeth 12 – 25.

Life moved along at its leisurely island pace, except for Kathy. The permitting process for bringing elk to Maui was long and involved, but she was making progress. Meanwhile, I'd become friends with an older gentleman, Reems Mitchell, an artist of sorts who lived in the ruins of a 17th century sugar mill on the ranch.

He had dragged all kinds of unique materials up the volcano to the mill, everything from bits of glass to the beams of sunken ships, and built a fanciful little home among the tall stone chimneys and crumbling walls. Few things fit so well in their surroundings as Mitch, a unique person and very funny guy.

We spent many tranquil afternoons on his front porch, laughing and enjoying an unobstructed view of the sparkling blue ocean and the island of Molokini. Mo also enjoyed going to Mitch's. His passion for herding cows would get him shot in a second on the ranch, so he spent most of his day hooked up. The visits with my friend were among the few times Mo got to be off his dog run.

When we were at Mitch's, Mo usually slept in the shade under the porch. One day when we were visiting I noticed a flock of sheep to the right of the ruins pick up their heads in unison and begin to move. I'd seen that reaction before. Sure enough, when I followed their gaze I found Mo low crawling through the grass a few hundred feet to our left. He was doing a great job of it, but was simply too big to go unnoticed. It would have been funny if he weren't committing a capital offense.

I stood up and yelled at Mo who immediately took off after the sheep. In an instant rage I leapt from my chair on an intercept course with the bounding hound.

Within seconds I'd closed the distance between us to a dozen yards. I yelled as loudly as I could for him to stop, but we were too close to the sheep, nothing was going to distract him. In fact, I believe Mo thought I was joining in on the fun. As he left me in his dust he glanced back and I swear the look he gave me said, "You go right, I'll go left," which he did. Of course Mitch thought the whole thing was hysterical. I had to laugh too.

More than a month after I opened my claim with the VA to have my dental situation reviewed, they sent a request for records from the hospitals that admitted me with intestinal strangulation, and reports from the doctors I'd seen. No mention of my teeth or dentists at all, which I assumed meant that the VA had all the information in their files they needed.

The doctor in Fairbanks who treated me the first time I threw up had left town, and the hospital in Juneau couldn't find the emergency room reports at first. It took almost a month, a surprising amount of time, but I finally got the information the VA requested and mailed it to them.

A week or two later I got a letter back stating my case had been closed, that I hadn't responded to their request for records in the allotted amount of time. When I called the VA and assured someone in the claims department that everything had been sent weeks ago, I was told, "things get lost," and that I should resubmit the information, which I did with "return receipt requested."

Several days later I called to see if the VA had received the records I'd resubmitted, and was told they hadn't. When I told them I had a signed return receipt, they said they'd look again. The next day someone from claims called to tell me they'd found the records and reports I'd sent in. It was almost unbelievable. Was it intentional? Could they actually function that way?

I'd gone from loving to loathing the Veterans Administration in a matter of months. I simply asked them to do the right thing. Take care of my teeth, pay for Rick, and cover surgery if it was necessary. These things were obviously related to combat; yet, from not signing or dating their correspondence to outright denying responsibility they seemed to be going out of their way to avoid helping me.

Kathy assured me it was just a case of gross ineptness in an oversized, under-funded agency. She agreed there might be a little impunity, but cautioned that I shouldn't take it personally.

As the weeks dragged on with no response from the VA about my claim, my anxiety rose. I began checking the mail every day. More than the dental issue, I was worried about being able to get surgery. The longer they put me off, the more I began to believe it might be necessary at any time.

Once again, I called the VA in Honolulu too see what progress they were making on my claim. The operator switched me to Dr. Vandervort, the director of the hospital. I told him my story and he assured me everything would be taken care of, that I should be patient, that things take time. So, I went back to waiting.

I'd been seeing my psychologist, and friend, Rick Sword all along. The VA had continued to pay for his services while my claim was being processed. When I told him about my concerns that the VA was dragging things out as long as they could, he told me, "Get use to it. Figure the time it should take, double it and add on a year or two. And forget about the dental. They won't do it. Too much of a long-term commitment and too expensive."

As for them paying for surgery to fix my adhesions. "Who knows about that kind of thing," Rick said. "Sometimes they jump right in and help you out. Other times they just leave you twisting in the wind. They screw over a lot of vets."

"I'm beginning to hate them," I blurted out.

"That's pretty common at this stage of the game. But it won't do you any good. What will help is this advice. They do follow a system of sorts. No matter how fucked up, you've got to learn how to operate within it, play by their rules. It's their sandbox," he finished sympathetically.

"Maybe," I agreed reluctantly. "But the only reason they're here is to help vets like me... guys wounded in combat."

"And all the other guys too," Rick reminded me. "But that's sort of gotten lost in the process somewhere. Anyway, a lot of the things you think are completely screwed are really just the way it's done. Go figure. But what you need to learn is to relax, take it easy and just keep going. It's not a matter of right or wrong when you deal with the VA," Rick said. "It's more of a last man standing kind of thing."

Not long after that informative session with Rick I got a letter from Oahu telling me to show up for a dental exam. After the appointment I believed I'd made a good case for teeth 12 – 25 instead of 12 & 25.

In the waiting room I struck up a conversation with the only other guy there. When I mentioned that the VA was being less than helpful with my dental problems, he said, "I know what you mean, man." Turning his head so I could see the other side of his face, he pointed to a large patch of scar tissue on his cheek. "AK round went in there and came out my mouth. Knocked half my teeth out but they won't give me dental either."

If the VA wouldn't help a guy who'd had his teeth knocked out by a bullet, what chance did I have? I was beginning to think that nothing I said would make any difference to them.

When a letter arrived from Honolulu a few weeks later, I felt a rush of relief; certain it was approval for surgery. I didn't care about the teeth any more, was willing to forgive everything if they'd just take care of my adhesions. The intermittent bouts of nausea were making me paranoid. I felt sure the Veterans Administration wasn't going to pay for the surgery when I needed it.

But the letter contained a bill for $176.00 from the oral surgeon the VA set me up with when my tooth was infected. The attached letter told me to pay it because only teeth 12 & 25 were covered. I laughed. In my military records from St. Louis I'd learned that those two teeth were somewhere in a jungle in Vietnam. Then I called Dr. Vandervort at the VA hospital.

He did a good job of pacifying me, agreeing that since

81

they'd authorized the extraction the VA should also cover the oral surgeon's bill. Then he went on to say, "In the future though, work on anything but teeth twelve and twenty-five won't be covered. You'll have to wait until the Adjudication Board settles your claim and service connects all your teeth. Once that's done, we'll gladly pay all the bills."

I didn't bother to tell him where those teeth were; however, since he was the hospital director I thought I'd ask him if he had any idea how my claim was going. "It's not just the dental part of the claim I'm worried about," I told him. "My adhesions are getting pretty bad, and I think it's about time to consider surgery."

"Well, first of all," Vandervort returned, "You'll have to talk to the Adjudication Board about your claim. They handle that. And as far as adhesions are concerned, you know they're in a gray area." When I didn't say anything because I was trying to digest what he'd said, he added. "I'm sure you've been told that they don't show up on X-rays that well."

"What the hell are you saying?" I got mad so fast I didn't even feel it coming.

"Adhesions aren't easily diagnosed," he replied nonchalantly.

"I know that," I replied, feeling the pressure build. "I've been to at least a dozen doctors. They've checked for everything else. The only thing it can be is adhesions. Dr. Buesa over here says he'll give me a referral for surgery. What more of a diagnosis do you need?"

"They may well be adhesions," the director said. "But until we know for sure . . ."

"Are you saying you're not going to pay for my surgery, until I can definitively prove something you just told me can't be proven?" I paused, but there was no response on the other end of the phone line. I was so upset I was trembling. "How can you find out they're adhesions without surgery? How the hell can you ask that of me?"

"I'm not saying anything, just trying to explain the process," he tried to reassure me.

"It seems to me that you're not doing anything," I replied, exasperated, and hung up the phone.

When I eventually calmed down, I felt totally lost. I knew it was only a matter of time before the adhesions kinked my intestines again and put me in the hospital. I also knew I would put surgery off as long as possible if I had to pay for it, increasing the chance of damaging my intestines. And Dr. Vandervort was telling me they'd have to think about it, had actually asked me to understand. I couldn't help but wonder how understanding he'd be in the same spot.

Later that day when I told Kathy what had happened, how the VA was treating me, her reaction blew me away. "It's hard to blame them sometimes," she said. "The way you yell and get so mad can turn anyone off."

Barely able to control my temper, I went outside and sat alone for hours, angry with everyone and feeling very sorry for myself. Gradually I realized that the director of the VA hospital wasn't to blame. Rick was right, there was a system that had to be followed. I'd have to wait for the Adjudication Board's decision.

Kathy was right too. She could have been more diplomatic, if not sympathetic, but she'd been putting up with my outbursts for a long time. If anyone could comment on my anger, it was Kathy. Also, she had a lot on her mind, and was less inclined to be her usual tolerant self. It appeared that the Department of Agriculture might approve her permit on the first draft, a remarkable feat, and she might well be bringing elk to Maui in a matter of months.

18

Six months after Kathy began the process, the State of Hawaii gave her permission to bring elk to Maui. One of the officials told her they didn't want to permit the project, but couldn't find a reason not to. She'd done too good of a job.

Construction on the elk enclosure began. Kathy bought miles of game fence from New Zealand and brought in a fencing crew from Montana to put it up. At the same time construction began on the 6,000 square foot handling facility.

While Kathy was getting the project underway, I decided it was time to do something about the adhesions on my intestines. I was tired of the paranoia. The bouts of nausea were more frequent, slowly growing worse, and I knew that life was going to get busier for both of us. So, having surgery sooner seemed better than later. I'd also decided not to wait for the VA's help. With Kathy's income we could pay it off over time if need be.

Dr. Buesa recommended getting the operation done on the mainland, so I began to ask around. My brother Norm, a lawyer in Boston, recommended the Lahey Clinic and offered to let me stay with him afterwards. I made an appointment to see one of their surgeons that coming fall.

Dr. Vandervort had been right about adhesions being hard to diagnose. Even the doctors at one of the best hospitals in the East couldn't say for certain I had them, and performed a bunch of tests on me just to make sure it wasn't something else. One I'll never forget was the small bowel biopsy.

They stood me in front of an X-ray screen and slid a quarter inch cable down my throat. Using the X-ray for guidance they worked the cable through my stomach into my duodenum and small intestine, then sniped a piece of tissue for a biopsy. The whole time they were doing the procedure tears ran down my cheeks in a steady stream while my gag reflex kicked in over and over again.

In the middle of November, six months after I opened my claim with the VA, I underwent elective surgery at the Lahey Clinic and put it on my credit card. Everything went fine. They found several adhesions among my intestines, which they removed.

The surgeon told me the scar tissue was secondary to the laparotomy performed in Vietnam and gave me a letter to that effect, which made me feel good, a vindication of sorts. Even more important, I didn't have to worry about puking up my guts anymore, or dying of intestinal strangulation. It had been the adhesions all along, and they were gone. I could even go back to flying if I wanted to.

Back in Hawaii, I sent Dr. Vandervort a copy of the surgeon's letter. He called me a few days later, thanked me for the letter and told me he'd forward it to the Adjudication Board. He also said that he thought the VA would pay for the surgery. By the time he hung up, my attitude towards the Veterans Administration had changed once more.

I really wanted to believe they were on my side until a few days later, when I got a letter from them saying, "This is just to let you know that we have received your application for benefits. There is no need for you to take any additional action at this time." It was déjà vu of the worst kind.

A month or so after surgery I was feeling better than I had in a long time and threw myself into working with Kathy on her project for the ranch. The fencing and the facility for handling the elk were well underway and she'd been calling about privately owned animals for sale in Canada and the US.

We flew to the mainland three times looking for the right animals before Kathy settled on 50 elk from a farm in the Midwest. Most of them came over on a chartered flight with horses bound for the islands. We unloaded them at night, down covered ramps into covered cattle trucks, and all went well. Half a dozen elk came from a different farm so Kathy and I had to make a separate trip.

We rented a U-Haul truck, built the shipping cages ourselves, loaded the elk and drove to Chicago where the animals were put in the cargo hold of a DC-10 heading to Maui. It got pretty tense when the makeshift elk containers barely cleared the hatch. The measurements the airline representative gave me were for a different airplane.

Close calls aside, all in all it was a tremendous accomplishment. An outfit in Texas that specialized in the transportation of exotic animals had told Kathy she should expect at least a 20% loss in the process.

As usual, having something to do was good for me, but long hours in the airplanes and rental cars brought on the same nausea I'd had before surgery. My adhesions were back, or possibly they were new ones, either way it was pretty depressing. I didn't like to think about the ramifications of their return, that surgery was no longer a certain cure, and flying helicopters was out, again.

Three months after my trip to the Lahey Clinic I still hadn't received a check from the VA for the cost of the operation, so I called Dr. Vandervort to make sure it hadn't gotten lost. He said that the Adjudication Board had the letter from the Lahey Clinic but couldn't give me any more information than that. When I asked him why it was taking so long, he replied, "In order to make an informed decision, the Board needs all the information it can get."

"I've sent them at least a dozen reports from as many doctors," I told him. I felt like yelling, how much more information do you need?

There was silence on the phone for a moment. "How many VA doctors have you seen?" Dr. Vandervort asked.

"Well. In VA hospitals?" I had to think. "It's been a long time."

"So, you've only been to your doctors?" he said, emphasizing "your." When I didn't get it right away, he added. "There's a big difference, you know."

"You mean?" As it sank in I felt more sick than angry. "You mean, all the stuff I've done, the doctors appointments, asking them to write letters, doesn't mean anything to the Board?"

"They read everything they get," the good doctor assured me. "However, they might attach more significance to doctors they know."

After the phone call, and when my anger subsided, I

86

realized Dr. Vandervort had done me a favor. He could have not said anything and let me waste more of my time. Later that day I made appointments with the dental clinic, the gastroenterologist, and an orthopedic doctor at the VA hospital in Honolulu. I also asked to see someone in the psychiatric department who specialized in PTSD.

In April, nearly a year after I'd opened my claim, I went to Honolulu to see the VA's doctors. After the appointments I requested a copy of their reports. The gastroenterologist was honest, described the healing incision from bellybutton to sternum as secondary to the laparotomy preformed in Vietnam. But that's where the credibility ended.

The dentist noted nine of my teeth were missing, without any explanation of how or why, but reaffirmed that only teeth 12 and 25 were service connected. The orthopedic doctor's report wasn't much better. He mentioned my back injuries and limited range of motion, but made a point of saying that I got around well. And the psychiatrist had taken the uncertainty I'd expressed about PTSD and turned it into a confession.

At that point I knew a number of people at the VA were trying to minimize, if not outright deny, my medical problems. I generally avoid rumors and conspiracy theories, but so many people seemed to be involved, I was beginning to believe my file was marked or something.

19

Several weeks after my visit to the VA's doctors on Oahu I got a letter informing me I had another appointment with their psychiatrist. I wasn't about to fly over there, go through the hassles of the airport and the risk of flying, just to see a shrink who lied about what I'd said to him.

When I told the Psychiatric Clinic's receptionist I wasn't coming over, and why, they made an appointment for me to see a psychiatrist on Maui named Henry.

By then I'd been seeing Rick on and off for more than a year. He was frustrated by my inability to see the role PTSD was playing in my life, and "to connect the dots" as he kept saying. I was getting tired of going over the same things with him. I still couldn't see how anything I experienced in the military could be causing problems seventeen years later. Consequently, seeing another doctor seemed like a good idea.

I didn't have a lot else to do. With work on the elk facility completed, I was back to house chores, taking long walks on the ranch with Mo, hanging out with Mitch, and exercising more than ever before.

It was almost masochistic the way I worked on aching joints and tissue, but I'd found that by putting up with the daily pain I avoided a lot of pulled muscles and pinched nerves. I also believed, for no apparent reason, that staying in shape would help me contend with my adhesions, possibly even my anger.

Life was fairly steady, other than the VA who continued to be a constant source of irritation. Most recently I got a letter from them requesting a copy of the surgery report from the Lahey Clinic. The same records I had sent seven or eight months earlier. I wanted to write the Board a letter detailing their ineptness, but knew that's not the way the system worked, so I sent another copy of the records they requested.

No more than a week later a letter came from the Adjudication Board. They had reached a decision in my claim. I couldn't believe it. When I least expected it, something actually happened.

In the Board's decision it rated my adhesions 10% disabling, and my back 30%. They also gave me 20% for PTSD. With the ratings combined I would be getting over $300.00 a month, which I thought was a decent amount of money. Also enclosed was a check that covered the cost of the operation at the Lahey Clinic

I appreciated the VA paying for the surgery, and really felt good about their giving me 30% for my back. I thought it was more than fair.

I'd been working on the elk facility and a few other odd jobs around the ranch, but reached my limit when it came to building a cinderblock wall. Lifting the heavy blocks of concrete did some serious damage and put my lower back muscles in spasms for weeks. Standing up took both hands. And the sciatic nerve in my left leg felt like a frayed cable flaying tissue from ankle to butt every time I moved. After that I vowed to never lift anything heavy ever again. That lasted until I felt better.

I thought the rating for PTSD was fair, mostly because it was something I didn't fully understand, but 10% for my adhesions was ridiculous. They cost me my career as a commercial pilot, and had a major impact on everything I'd done since. Also, the Board hadn't even mentioned dental, which was what started the whole thing.

On the last page of the Adjudication Boards rating decision there was an appeals process. Without much deliberation I sent the VA a "notice of disagreement," seeking a higher rating for the "residuals of adhesions," as they termed the scar tissue on my intestines. I also asked specifically for all my teeth to be service connected.

Their response was fast. "This is just to let you know that we have received your application for benefits. There is no need for you to take any additional action at this time." The process was beginning again, the requests for information, doctors' reports, everything. The thought of it made me tremble with frustration, then rage. I called Dr. Vandervort and gave him such a hard time I felt compelled to write a letter of apology the next day.

A week or two later a letter came from the VA's Vocational Rehabilitation office. My initial reaction was to throw it out. The Veterans Administration was driving me nuts. Why would I want to get more involved? But I'd read something about preferential hiring of vets, and thought the Voc Rehab people might be able to help me find a new career.

The councilor was a nice guy, but all he had to work with were some placement tests and the help-wanted ads in the local paper. When it became apparent that Vocational Rehabilitation wasn't going anywhere, I came to the disconcerting realization that income, as I'd know it, was a thing of the past. I had gone from a well-paid helicopter pilot to a vocational rehab dropout.

At that point it wasn't only the throwing up, my bad back, or the inability to get along with people that was holding me down. I'd become detached, disconnected. I had always been able to look at things from different perspectives, see the options, and find my way through life. After Voc Rehab, it was as if I'd had a lobotomy. I couldn't see anything worth doing, and didn't seem to care. The attitude that got things going, the will that got them done, was gone.

It was definitely a low point in my life. Then I noticed the familiar taste of infection in my mouth. A trip to the dentist confirmed that tooth 19 was abscessed. A call to the Veterans Administration confirmed its position that 19 wasn't service connected, and that I'd have to open a claim if I wanted that changed. Around then Dr. Vandervort stopped accepting or returning my calls.

Ten months after I appealed the Adjudication Board's first rating decision, they came back with another one. The Board raised the rating for adhesions to 30% disabling, the same as my back, and finally addressed the issue of dental coverage.

"The veteran's contentions as to his dental condition were noted and a review of all records applicable to his dental problem was made. There is no basis by which service connection for teeth 12 and 25 could be reversed to include other teeth." In closing they added, "As this award grants the benefit sought, your notice of disagreement is considered withdrawn."

I couldn't believe the audacity of the Adjudication Board, telling me they'd granted the benefit sought right after telling me dental was denied. I wasn't about to withdraw my notice of disagreement. I had to pay to get tooth 19 removed.

Working with the Veterans Administration was not easy, definitely the darker side of my life around then. When I wasn't dealing with them though, things were still pretty good. I'd gotten over the whole thing with Vocational Rehabilitation, about being a failure. How could I consider myself a failure when I was living on Maui and my wife had good job.

But what made life really enjoyable, was Kathy. When the tirades came to an end, when the anger left my heart, she was there. It was similar to a high-speed elevator coming to a stop, and the doors open onto green fields and sunshine. She was the best thing in my life, and also becoming a legend on the ranch.

On her way to the elk enclosure one morning she ran into several of the ranch cowboys working on a fence. They told Kathy that a wild boar, the same one that had been coming around trying to get at the elk food, was back again; and that the pig was in the enclosure tearing up fences and spooking her animals.

The wild pigs on Maui are nasty looking creatures, with big heads, massive chests, and two long teeth protruding from their lower jaws.

Kathy thanked the cowboys for the information and headed up the mountain on her four-wheeler. At the handling facility she picked up her revolver, the Blackhawk .44 magnum she carried in Alaska. Kathy kept it around in case an animal was injured and might have to be put down. Then she got back on her ATV and went after the pig. There was no getting the animal out of the enclosure any other way.

Not wanting to get mauled by the beast, Kathy stopped her four-wheeler more than 200 feet away, stood up on the foot pegs, and took aim for the big boar's heart. The first shot hit him high on the shoulder, the second in the leg. That's when he decided to fight. As he charged, Kathy emptied her revolver. The bullet that brought him down caught him in the eye.

She didn't have time to do anything with the dead pig because of a meeting at the ranch office. When she passed the cowboys on her way down the mountain, she asked them if they'd dispose of the carcass for her; knowing they would take the big boar home and cook it. After that the cowboys had nothing but respect for the Elk Lady, as they called her.

Everyone on the ranch liked Kathy, and she deserved it, but her success highlighted my failure. If the cowboys had a name for me it was most likely House Man.

Almost daily they caught me going about my domestic chores, on my way in with the groceries, sweeping the porch or hanging laundry. I didn't mind. Those things had to be done and it beat doing nothing, or sitting around feeling sorry for myself. However, from where the cowboys sat on their handsome ponies, I must have looked pretty pathetic, which may have had something to do with what happened next.

Kathy had a habit of picking up baby sheep in the pastures she crossed on her way home from the elk enclosure, particularly during storms. When the wind driven rain spooked the ewes, they often left their lambs behind. The ones under a week old or so couldn't keep up and faced certain death on their own; so, we fed the baby sheep until they were strong enough to live on grass. We found that, generally, the younger they were, the higher their survival rate. Little lambs still in their natal jelly seemed to have an incredible will to survive.

I believe they fought harder because they hadn't become dependent on their mothers. The lambs had not learned to rely on anyone else. This led me to believe the Spartans may have had it right. They took their trainees at seven. Maybe, like the newborn lambs, their child soldiers were tougher for it.

One evening Kathy came home with an older animal. The ewe was sick and not using her front legs, actually starving to death because she couldn't forage farther than the reach of her neck.

"The darn thing was right there by the gate for two days," Kathy told me. "Not getting any better or worse. Every time I went by I'd prop her up, but she kept falling over. And those big, pathetic eyes... God I hate that," she finished, as I helped her lift the mangy critter off the front rack of the four-wheeler and lay it on the ground. Sure enough, the animal couldn't stand up.

We kept the ewe alive for a month or two by picking her up

and moving her around the lawn. Kathy also gave her medicine and special supplements, but she didn't regain the use of her legs. Finally we had to admit that we were just prolonging the crippled animal's misery.

I would have volunteered for the nasty job of putting the ewe down; however, with the problems I'd been having with intrusive thoughts, I didn't think shooting a nice old sheep in the head was such a good idea.

Kathy said she'd take care of it, but kept postponing the dirty deed. When I realized she didn't want to kill the ewe any more than I did, I decided to do it for her sake and mine. For at least two years it seemed that all I'd done was whine and complain about my problems. It was about time I did something noble.

My choice of weapons was a 12-gauge shotgun or our .22 target pistol. I thought the shotgun would be pretty messy, so after loading the pistol with nine rounds I went out to the pen to put her down.

I wasn't sure exactly where the sheep's brain was, so I put the muzzle a few inches from her forehead and pulled the trigger. There was a loud pop and we both flinched. Then we were looking at each other.

The bullet had hit where I'd aimed, but she wasn't dead by any stretch of the imagination. So I shot her again. That didn't kill her either. Goddamn it, I said to myself, and tried the back of her head, pulling the trigger until the gun was empty.

It was a nightmare. She was still alive, looking at me with blood running out of the corner of her mouth. Out of ammo, completely flustered and feeling terrible about what I was putting the old girl through, I picked up the shovel I used to dig her grave and hit her on the head as hard as I could, and then again because she didn't even fall over, just sat there looking straight ahead.

The third time she went down and I pulled the ewe into her grave, but it wasn't over. Half covered with dirt she began to move, and I had to hit her on the head one more time to finally kill her.

When Kathy got home from work she already knew what had happened. Evidently the cowboys were at the holding pen across the road and told her I'd been shooting a gun at the house. She figured out the rest.

"But, nine shots?" she asked. "That must have been awful," she said, genuinely sorry for me. "Are you sure you're all right?"

I wanted to tell her that life was good, I was fine, but I couldn't. "No," I told her, as a deep sadness washed over me. "I'm not all right."

20

We had been on Maui for two years when Kathy suggested we take a vacation. Maybe spend Christmas and New Year's on the mainland. I hadn't thought about it, but when she brought it up I couldn't think of anything I needed more than a nice long road trip.

We crossed the country seeing family and friends. It felt like a vacation. I was enjoying everything. The trip ended in the Adirondack Mountains for a peaceful Christmas with my brothers and sister.

When we got back to Hawaii, house cleaning and exercising didn't fill up my day the way they once did. I wanted something else, anything that would keep me from slipping back into the rut I'd been in before we went on vacation. Once again, Kathy suggested I write a book. She even bought me a computer. "Give it a try," she said.

For a subject, I chose Vietnam. There had been a renewal of interest in the war, and I figured my scout pilot experiences would make a good story. But I came close to giving up on the project within days.

Sitting for hours at a desk made my back muscles spasm. My sciatic nerves didn't like it either. Then I found a kneeling chair at an office supply store. Distributing my weight between my butt and knees made a big difference to my back, and a gel pad placated my sciatica.

It didn't take long for me to realize how much I liked writing. Almost immediately I got caught up in the challenge of getting ideas down and managing words. My mind became engrossed in what I was doing. Writing had one of the steepest learning curves I'd encountered. It was the perfect distraction.

Days, then months went by, as I got deeper into my life as a scout pilot. One evening I closed my eyes and held an image of myself sitting as I was, but on my cot in Tay Ninh. I didn't let it go and thought of nothing else, picturing every detail I could remember. Before long I was there. I could see it, smell it, and even feel it. It wasn't weird. I actually felt very comfortable, relaxed. It had been my home, on the other side of the world and almost beyond memory.

While I was writing I seldom thought about the Veterans Administration. When I got requests for something like a doctor's report or another certified copy of our marriage certificate, things that use to drive me nuts, I just did it as quickly as I could to get back to my book.

For a break I began walking with Mo in the middle of the day. Within a month I was running again with my big dog at my side. The ranch roads were a soft volcanic soil, which made it easy on my back.

The exercise was good for my health and facilitated writing. I'd forgotten how well the rhythmic footfalls and deep breathing brought organization and clarity to my thoughts. After a three-mile run I knew exactly where the story would go that day.

Life was as good as it had been in a long time. Even my angst-ridden VA mentality had changed. I saw my arch nemesis/mentor in a less antagonistic light. Maybe the impersonal nature of our contact is creating problems, I thought, considering how the Adjudication Board only saw letters and doctors' statements.

I knew there was such a thing as a hearing with the Board and decided that meeting them would give me a chance to explain why I kept appealing their decisions. It would also be an opportunity for them to tell me why they were denying me dental care.

A fellow veteran told me I should get a service officer from one of the veterans' groups on the island to go to the hearing with me. That was their job he said, to represent vets, protect them from the VA.

It couldn't hurt, I figured, and got in touch with Vince Cui of the Disabled American Veterans. He was a great guy who'd been helping vets for more than a decade. Vince thought I should be getting more for my back and PTSD, but not for my dental problems. "They don't do that," he told me.

That summer Kathy, Vince and I flew to Oahu for a personal hearing with the people I'd been in contention with for almost three years. However, we actually met with an assistant of the Board, and the direct contact I'd sought ended up being a typewritten transcript of our conversation.

Even so, Kathy and I thought the hearing went well. The evidence we submitted was from the VA's own doctors. Their letters included things like "degenerative disc disease," "incapacitated," and "compulsive personality disorder." Once again I got to present evidence that more than teeth 12 & 25 were injured when I was shot down.

The Adjudication Board gave me a 10% increase in PTSD, which I hadn't asked for, and to my utter disbelief cut my back condition from 30 to 20%, stating that I had good range of motion. They didn't even mention dental. Sons' of bitches, I thought, ready to file another notice of disagreement, until I read the last line of the rating decision.

If I wanted to appeal the Adjudication Board's final decision, I would have to go the Board of Veterans Appeals in Washington, D. C. I had thirty days in which to decide. I called Vince and asked what we could do. "Not much," was his response. Anything we tried at the local level would just make enemies of his counterparts at the VA, people he had to work with every day. "Better to go to Washington," he told me.

A week later I got a letter from the VA on Oahu. "Dear Mr. Smith," it read. "On June 17th we requested that you furnish the following evidence: Certified Marriage Certificate. Since you did not respond to our previous letter, we must disallow your claim."

I was beyond anger, and sent them another copy of the certificate, wondering how much longer I could put up with the frustration. A few days after that, the VA notified me they weren't going to pay for private psychiatrists or psychologists anymore.

Not being able to see Henry, the private psychiatrist the VA set me up with on Maui, didn't bother me. He and I weren't getting along. Henry thought I was cocky, and I knew he was an egotist.

Near the end of our final session he told me that I might want to consider admitting myself to a VA hospital for inpatient psychiatric care. I was amazed how little he knew about me. Just the thought of being incarcerated made me cringe.

I didn't give his suggestion a second thought, but his not-so-subtle appraisal of my mental condition raised a question. "If you think I should commit myself. Do you think I'm crazy?" I asked Henry.

"No," he answered. "But you can use some help."

"Do you think I'm dangerous?" I persisted. Recently, in a moment of rage, I considered going to Oahu with my shotgun to get their attention. It wasn't a rational thought, more of a last resort, pissed off impulse. But I could feel my mindset begin to change, the world close in, become dark and dangerous. Don't be an idiot, I'd told myself.

"What exactly do you mean?" he asked.

"You know," I replied. "Do you think I could really lose it? Maybe hurt someone?"

Henry thought for a minute. "No," he told me. But a second later, he added, "Unless something were to happen to Kathy."

That made sense.

Not being able to see Henry didn't bother me; however, having the Veterans Administration take the benefit away made it impossible to get psychiatric counseling, unless I wanted to fly to the VA hospital on Oahu each time. But why... to save money? That didn't make sense. The cost of the airplane ticket alone was more than a local doctor's fee.

Sometime after my last visit with Henry, I had to decide whether or not I wanted to appeal the VA's rating decision at the Board of Veterans Appeals in Washington D.C. I was tired of the game, would rather stick with my writing and just forget about them. However, they had lied to me, treated me like shit, and still hadn't service connected my teeth.

As soon as the appeal was in the mail I slipped back into the solace of writing. I had several chapters by then and was ready for an unbiased opinion. Kathy was hesitant, but I insisted.

"What do you think?" I asked when she finally finished. I was expecting an enthusiastic response, but she was obviously uncomfortable.

"Well, I wasn't there," she began.

"Okay," I said. "But what do you think of my writing?"

I couldn't believe the way she was avoiding talking about it. Finally she said, "I'm sorry, Tom. But it's really pretty bad."

I completely lost it. Infuriated I told her how little she knew about writing, or anything for that matter, and then stormed out of the house. When I came back, I tersely explained that it was just a beginning. Later that evening I asked her what the problem was.

"It's not entertaining," she explained. "It's angry, bitter. You've got to lighten up. Just tell the story as if you were talking to some friends in the bar."

As soon as I sat down to write the next day I appreciated what Kathy had done for me. I could see my story as its own entity, not an extension of me. From then on Kathy helped keep me on course, which I appreciated, but that didn't stop me from blowing up regularly. I couldn't help it. Writing is personal and my anger was never far below the surface.

Four years after Kathy went to work for the ranch, I wanted to move. I wanted to go back to the Adirondack Mountains and live there again, maybe forever. I loved the ranch, Kathy's job was great, and it was a nice place to write, but the desire to go home kept growing.

Before long I was dropping hints to Kathy. At first it was jokes, like, "Things are going great, so it must be time to move." Then I tried reason. "You know. If I want to do a good job on that appeal to the VA in Washington, it would be easier to do it if we were back there."

One day, after a similarly lame attempt, Kathy surprised me. "I'll have to find someone good to take care of my elk," she said nonchalantly.

"You mean you'd actually consider moving?" I asked, amazed. Kathy had never expressed an interest in living anywhere near the densely populated East coast.

"I've thought about it, too" she admitted. "You're being so subtle helped a lot, of course. But the truth is, things are changing. The hardest part of the job's done, getting the animals set up and on a healthy diet. Now it's the marketing part, selling the animals to people around the world. I know it's going to worry me where they go, and how they'll be treated."

"That will be tough," I agreed.

"And the ranch is looking into selling meat to some of the

restaurants in Wailea." She knew every one of her animals, picking one for slaughter would not be easy. "Maybe it's time to let someone else take over. As you said, everything's perfect so it's probably time to go."

Before leaving Hawaii we decided to take a trip to Alaska. It had been almost five years since we'd been back, and New York would be even further away. I had expected to enjoy every minute of the excellent trip we'd planned; after all, I loved Alaska and we were traveling. But I was stressed the whole time. I didn't want to be there. I wanted to get on with my life. Every day was a delay.

After sailing around Glacier Bay for a week with some friends, and camping on Kodiak Island on our own, Kathy and I went to Fairbanks. We floated the Chena River, something we frequently did together when we lived there, and I got very drunk. In a nice restaurant later that evening I went too far, verbally abusing people I didn't know, saying things to Kathy that were unforgivable.

When I woke up in a friend's apartment the next morning, and remembered what I'd done the night before, I shuddered. First things first, I told myself. I needed some water. Kathy woke up as I climbed back into bed. "Sorry about last night," I said.

"You're lucky I'm still here," she returned in a voice devoid of emotion.

"I know," I replied, apologetically. "That's why I'm quitting drinking."

On my way to the kitchen to get the glass of water, I went by our camping gear from the trip to Kodiak. Leaning against our packs were the shotguns we carried for self-defense. I looked at mine and dispassionately thought about shooting myself, could feel the twelve-gauge in my hands. Similar to the time I thought about taking my gun to the VA facility in Hawaii, I also felt my mindset begin to change, the world began to close in, the isolation deepen.

With a conscious effort I kept walking; telling myself it was an intrusive thought, or maybe a rational attempt to escape some serious pain. Either way, I didn't like where it was heading. In fact, I didn't want to get that drunk, or be that hung over, ever again, and decided to quit drinking.

"Okay. That's a start," Kathy said with very little enthusiasm.

"For a year," I continued. "And if I ever get drunk again, I'm quitting forever."

She studied me for a moment. Then asked, "Why?"

After I told her about the shotgun in the living room she gave me a kiss, took my empty glass, and said, "I'll get you some more water."

SUICIDAL DEPRESSION

The feeling that life would be better in the mountains of Upstate New York was the driving force behind my need to leave beautiful Hawaii. I believed it was time to be on my own land, among old friends and good memories, in a place with little outside influence, where life would be more secure and manageable. I also believed there would be fewer triggers for my anger.

That's what concerned me the most those days, my anger. The adhesions limited what I could do; same with the back, but my anger, the constant intense outbursts were poisoning my life on a daily basis.

Ideally, moving to the small town would make it easier to isolate the things that made me mad, an environment that would allow me to identify and deal with them on an individual basis. If nothing else I figured that just getting away from the Veterans Administration in Hawaii would be good for me. Dealing with them had been drawn-out torture with endless waiting periods between grateful highs of hope and lows of loathing.

Only weeks after we moved back East I believed it was working. I all but forgot about the VA. If I thought about them at all, it was the scheduled appearance before the Board of Veterans Appeals in Washington. I was actually looking forward to that, even after the ineffective personal appearance before the Adjudication Board in Hawaii.

I was hoping that, because it was a different venue, the Board of Appeals in Washington would see things differently. If there was a conspiracy it was highly unlikely the Board would be part of it. And if the problem were, as Kathy maintained, simple bureaucratic ineptness, the highest authority in the Veterans Administration would certainly recognize incompetence for what it was, and correct the problem. Maybe they would even give me dental.

With little to worry about, we spent most of our time taking it easy, hiking, biking, swimming, and working around the house. We also did a lot of sleeping, often staying in bed until the smell of pine needles warming in the sun came through the open windows.

Life in the valley was even better with Kathy for company. I went to the same bars, saw the same people, but with her along it was different. I always had a good time, often got home at a reasonable hour, and seldom felt remorse. With neither of us working, our days fell together in response to the situation at hand. We enjoyed the peaceful surroundings and each other's company. Mo was particularly glad we had moved. Without cows to run, he was free to go where he wanted.

Before long there was a chill in the night air, then the mornings and evenings. We settled into the routines of fall, finishing outdoor projects and putting up firewood. The old summerhouse we were in wasn't insulated. One entire side was glass. So we knew we were going to burn a lot of wood.

By the time the leaves began to wither and fall we'd been back East nearly four months, and I could count the number of rages I'd had on one hand. I was beginning to think my life might be turning around... until I almost shot one of the men from town.

I came home one afternoon to find a pickup parked on the side of our driveway within sight of the house. I didn't recognize the truck, but it was the end of hunting season and fresh snow was on the ground. I figured it was someone trying to get in one last hunt on a good day for tracking.

Nevertheless, the thought of a guy I didn't know walking around our home with a loaded gun made me very uncomfortable, and parking on our land without permission pissed me off.

After leaving my car at the house I wrote a nasty note to leave at his truck. As I lifted the windshield wiper to slip it underneath, two loud reports from a high-powered rifle shattered the silence. Dropping to the ground, I cringed. By the sound of the report, the rifle was pointed in my direction.

The shots had come from the tree-covered slope to my left, so I scrambled around the vehicle to the other side. He's trying to scare me away from his pickup, I thought, as my fear flashed to rage. Son of a bitch, I said to myself, as I got up and ran towards the house. The back door flew open before I got there. Kathy had my twelve-gauge pump in her hands.

"It's loaded with slugs. One in the chamber," she said, handing me the shotgun and some spare shells. "I heard the shots," she added in response to my inquiring look. What a great girl, I thought.

When I got back to the truck I began screaming curses at the top of my lungs, telling the hunter I was coming after him, as I emptied the magazine into the woods where I thought he was. Then I reloaded and began following the tracks that left the truck, only to find that they led away from where the shots were fired.

It turned out that the guy who shot at me wasn't a rogue hunter, but someone from town whom I knew quite well. He was walking an old logging road on the hillside behind the truck when a large buck walked between us. It was too much to resist and he took the shot. The deer bolted and he squeezed off one more. Both shots missed the deer and were aimed right were I was standing at the time.

Later, the man from town told me the sounds of my slugs tearing through the trees all around him was terrifying, but I didn't feel sorry for him at all. He shouldn't have been shooting a gun that close to my home. However, my reaction was revealing.

Unleashing my rage, screaming and shooting up the forest, felt good. Not far below the surface there was a reservoir of anger, and my outburst had been a release. I hadn't noticed the pressure build, but I certainly felt it let go.

A few days later I called the Veterans Administration and asked them to set me up with a psychologist. They made an appointment for me with a psychiatrist in Plattsburgh, the nearest town of any size. The 50-mile trip each way wasn't worth the drive. His basement office smelled of damp concrete and stale cigarette smoke. As a family counselor, he had absolutely no experience with combat veterans. The only thing I got out of the first session was a profound sense of gratitude that I wasn't him.

The VA didn't have anyone else it worked with in the area, so I went to the guy in Plattsburgh again. Then the VA sent a letter saying I would have to drive to their regional hospital for psychiatric help. It was more than four hours round trip, but it had to be done. I had shot at a guy, intentionally and repeatedly, and thought I should talk to someone about it.

The psychiatrist at the VA hospital was a bright woman, but I only saw her a few times. When I told her about my anger, how deep and strong it was, the way it poisoned me, and was ruining my life, she wasn't interested. When I told her about the hunter, and my fears that there was a lot more where that came from, she gave me a quizzical look and suggested I check into one of the inpatient programs.

I didn't miss the psychiatrist, or her work environment. The regional hospital was one of the most depressing places I've ever been. In the lobby, waiting for my first appointment, I noticed a man who had a tracheotomy. I was close enough to hear the wheezing sound as air passed in and out of the little metal hole in his neck. I felt sorry for him until he took out a cigarette, stuck it in the tracheotomy hole and lit it.

The receptionist couldn't get my name to match my social security number, and the orthopedic doctor missed half of what I said because his English was, as he put it, "Not so good". Later that day they gave me a voucher for lunch. At the door of the cafeteria I had to walk around a pale old man in a wheelchair. The smell of urine was so strong I gagged.

After that I began crossing the border into Vermont for my basic health care. The outpatient clinic in Burlington was exactly what a VA clinic should be, small, clean, efficient, and well staffed by pleasant people. The regional hospital in White River Junction was old but well maintained, with patients clean and as happy as you'd expect, as well as having decent food.

At the VA hospital they set me up with a well-trained psychologist, and sent me to their physical therapist for help with back strengthening exercises. They even addressed some of my more vague complaints, like the issue with my legs.

Every now and then, for no apparent reason, one of my knees buckled. I always felt something like a mild shock in my lower back, and then a knee would just let go. I never hit the ground, but it was awkward. Fortunately it didn't happened that often. When I told the people in Vermont about it, they scheduled an electromyogram. They told me it was a way of measuring dissymmetry in nerve impulses.

I didn't feel good about the EMG from the beginning. Hospitals make me nervous, and I always feel vulnerable in those flimsy hospital gowns that open in the back, but when the doctor came in and picked up a cork with a thin wire protruding from it, my anxiety turned to fear.

"Are you ready?" he asked.

"For what?" I returned, eyeing the wire warily as he pulled the gown up to expose my thigh. Without waiting for an answer, he slowly pushed an inch of the wire into the upper part of my leg. "What the . . ." I gasped in pain. "God damn, that hurts," I told him, trying hard not to shout as he shoved the wire a little deeper.

"Not to be trite," he told me with a mirthless smile. "That's what they all say." Then he picked up another cork and pushed the wire into the calf of the same leg. The EMG report indicated some nerve disparity and recommended more tests, which I declined.

At home I split my time between writing, cross-country skiing and keeping the wood stove stoked. We burned 15 cords of wood and nearly 1,000 gallons of fuel oil before winter was over. Our house was so leaky and cold that there were little frost glaciers at the bottom of the windows, on the inside. I worked on my book in boots and a parka.

It was a survival situation, so when the time came for us to leave for Washington and my appointment with the Board of Veterans Appeals, I was ready to go. I was looking forward to the opportunity to present my case one more time, and it was also spring in the nation's capital. I needed some warm weather.

Cherry trees were budding, birds singing and, other than stumbling into the middle of a crack-house bust shootout a few blocks from our hotel, everything went well for us in the big city. At the hearing we were introduced to the four members of the Board and had to raise our right hands to take an oath. I went over the issues in detail. Then it was Kathy's turn.

Over the years Kathy and I had discussed PTSD and its symptoms from every possible angle, but as she responded to the questions put before her, I saw another picture. The following question and answer are from the transcript of the hearing:

Dr. Edwards to Mrs. Smith:

Q.   Mrs. Smith, is there anything that you have noticed that consistently triggers your husband's flare-up?

A.   Special things? Well, anything in any possible way perceived as threatening, yes. Any critical statement from any other person. Any situation where Tom doesn't feel 100 percent in control. If you tell him he's wrong. If he's challenged in any way or just put in a situation. Like, this has been traumatic coming here just walking down the streets of D.C. I've noticed we've been making sure we're back at the hotel well before dark. He just starts walking really fast and I've had to pull him back from the street corners when there are cars going by because he stops seeing, he stops focusing and keeps going. Because things like that set him off. They stimulate him. They charge him up and it takes him a while to wind down and you have to kind of remind him, talk to him. He'll talk himself down but a door slams or something dashes by or anything that moves—you know, Tom reacts like that. He reacts to things real fast and directionally, often inappropriately. Just very little things set him off. I'm trying to think of particular instances but really what we've done is adjusted our lifestyle. We've moved back to a very small town where his family is from for four generations and everyone knows Tom, and everyone is very accepting. We know our friends. They are old friends that he had from before Vietnam, the kids that he grew up with and we keep it that way. It's nice and simple. Also, Tom and I are best friends. We get along very well. We do just about everything together all the time and that makes it pretty easy but—you know, I'm sort of always on guard because he's always upset and always on guard. I'm always trying to think one step ahead of him—like how's this situation going to set Tom off? If I can, I'll steer myself into the middle of it, to avert it, because it's a lot easier to steer around things than to have Tom get in over his head. This sort of makes me the mother hen and all that, and I don't

108

like being in that position, but sometimes it's necessary. We found if he does his exercises religiously every morning that helps him. That little bit of physical release, that little bit of stretching and bending and we try to get out and walk a lot. I think PTSD's aggravated by physical conditions. When Tom's feeling bad he's more reactionary. He's more defensive and he's also more reactionary. That's all tied into the loss of control. When he doesn't feel you can do everything he wants you to do, or do things for himself, it upsets him and makes him upset with other people. That's all tied in together, both the mental and the physical—you know, it's hard to draw the line. And a lot of it, also, is that Tom just doesn't conceive that he has these problems. These last two years he's really just begun to...

While Kathy was talking to the members of the Board about me, I saw her in a different light. Until then I thought I was the sole authority on PTSD, the one who knew the most about it, had the experience. But that disappeared as I listened to my wife describe how she had to be on guard all the time.

I realized I wasn't the only one living with the disorder all day every day, and saw how much of her time and energy went into dealing with my symptoms. I couldn't help but wonder how long it had been since Kathy had been free to be herself.

Through her eyes I could also see my form of denial clearly. The way I coped with my problems, worked around them instead of dealing with them.

The members of the Board of Appeals listened intently through the twenty-four talking points I'd prepared, with accompanying attachments. They also appeared to be interested in what Kathy had to say. One of them was even a doctor. He had to understand what I'd been going through. When the Chairman said they would review the records thoroughly, I felt he meant it.

When spring came to the mountains I put aside my writing and began looking for work. Most of the jobs in the area were seasonal, which was fine with me. I hadn't had a lot of luck working fulltime.

Within days I found what I was looking for. I was hired by the town to eradicate the biting black flies that showed up that time of year. The work involved treating the water where the bugs bred, walking up to ten miles a day in the mountains, climbing and descending thousands of feet, and using dead reckoning to find my way around the trail-less valleys.

With each passing day in the woods I felt a little better, had fewer spasms and pulled muscles as my body grew stronger from the rigorous hikes. I rarely worried about my adhesions or anything else. Also, there was absolutely no one to get mad at.

As my life continued to improve, I could see that Kathy's was going the other way. She seemed restless a lot of the time, and wasn't enjoying things the way she used to. When I asked what was up, she told me she was feeling worthless and wanted to find something to do, but there just weren't any jobs.

One gray rainy day on Interstate 89, a month or so later, Kathy broke an unusually long period of silence, saying, "I can't remember a time I've been more down."

She sounded depressed. When I glanced over, Kathy was staring out the rain-streaked windshield. I was worried and wanted to say something reassuring. "I'm sorry, sweetheart, what…"

Before I could finish, she added, "I'm really just plain bummed."

Then Kathy turned and faced me. She looked pale, tired. My concern deepened. She just told me she was depressed, doing nothing with her life. What about a vacation, I thought. A week or two on an island somewhere might distract her from whatever it was that was bothering her. Pictures of white sand and drinks with umbrellas came into focus. "What about going..." I began.

"I can't find a job," Kathy said cutting me off again. She was looking out the window at nothing, seemingly unaware I was even talking to her. "I'm not doing anything constructive, can't think of anything meaningful or worthwhile to do. That's what's so discouraging."

"If it's something I can . . ."

"I've been thinking about having a baby," Kathy said, looking at me again, a strange mix of emotions in her eyes. "I might as well be a housewife, and look after kids."

"What?" I laughed, not sure I'd heard her correctly.

I thought we'd decided not to have kids. Six years earlier, while we were building the garage in the pasture on Maui, before PTSD was an issue, I had seriously considered children.

Nearing forty and thirty respectively, I thought we were both the right age. And if we were ever going to do it, living in a pasture in the tropics would be convenient when it came to diaper management. As they say on the island, "no need."

My deliberations must have shown because Kathy told me I was making her nervous; that, when I was working on the building I reminded her of a bird building a nest. After some discussion, but knowing all along the one with the womb would win, we agreed that having a family wasn't part of the plan.

"I'm not kidding," she sighed. "It's been bugging me for months and won't go away." After a short pause, she added. "If I had to guess, I'd say my biological clock is at work here." Then she looked at me, smiled, and appeared to be herself again.

A few weeks later I got some bad news. In a letter, the Board of Veterans Appeals in Washington unanimously agreed with the Veterans Administration in Hawaii. I was stunned. The three members of the Board seemed so rational, opened-minded and fair. How could they have overlooked so many facts, the opinions of all the professionals and their statements supporting my claims?

Only one thing made sense at that point; it had to be me. Either I was expecting too much, thought I deserved more than I was entitled to, or for reasons I couldn't comprehend, a fair number of people in the VA disliked me personally. I felt the will to fight leave my body. Disappointment, or maybe just fatigue, filled the void. But as I continued to read the letter from the Board of Veterans Appeals, I began to get angry, then madder than I'd been in a long, long time.

The evidence the Board of Veterans Appeals used in its "finding of fact" was even more selective than that of the VA in Hawaii. Whereas the Adjudication Board in Honolulu had merely ignored pertinent facts, the Board of Veterans Appeals, through inequitable comparisons and deliberate distortion, had gone out of its way to discount and discredit the conclusions of their own doctors.

Roger Bauer, chairman of the Board of Veterans Appeals actually wrote, "Classifications by physicians such as 'severe or moderate to severe' are not controlling upon the Board in applying the Rating Schedule."

The Board summed up its review of my appeal with, "While his disabilities may restrict the types of employment he can comfortably pursue, we do not find that they are of such severity as to preclude a person with his education and work experience from all forms of gainful employment."

I couldn't see how getting thrown out of college constituted an educational asset. Or how a disastrous career in real estate, not being able to fly, and numerous other short-term employment failures, could be counted as marketable experience.

The pricks, I said to myself. They seemed like such reasonable people. Then it dawned on me. It was right there, "gainful employment." That's what it was all about... unemployability. They didn't want to pay me 650 dollars a month for being unemployed.

So it had always been about money, as I often suspected. The funny thing was, I couldn't remember opening a claim for unemployability.

In my initial claim I mentioned that I had to quit flying helicopters because of my adhesions, but that was to get financial assistance for surgery. The other times I brought up work, it always related to my back or adhesions, not unemployability. Furthermore, I had a job, part time for the town, but still a job.

Why would I ask for unemployability from the VA when I wasn't even asking for unemployment benefits from the state?

As I sat, completely overwhelmed and feeling powerless, my anger began to subside. They were the last ones standing. Rick Sword had said it would come to that. It would end with the last one standing. Maybe it's for the best, I thought. The VA had been driving me nuts for years. I should be glad it was over. Then I saw "Appeals Notice" halfway down the page in front of me.

I was certain I'd been told the Board of Veterans Appeals in Washington was my last chance, so I read on. The notice said the recently formed United States Court of Veterans Appeals, a federal court that was not a part of the Veterans Administration, was hearing appeal cases that hadn't been decided by the VA before November 1988.

My case fell into that category. I was eligible, so I read it again. The court was completely independent of the Veterans Administration. It was almost incomprehensible... the thought of a real court after so many years of dealing with the duplicitous VA. My hopes rose cautiously, and then soared.

The United States Court of Veterans Appeals! Just the sound of it was inspiring. A real federal court bound by the laws of the land, not the policies of bureaucrats preserving their soulless organization.

As the thought settled in, I could literally see a judge asking the VA's attorney what the hell he meant by, "classifications by physicians are not controlling." How could they explain that doctors' reports don't mean anything when it comes to medical issues?

Just as quickly, the euphoria faded. How many times had I gotten my hopes up for nothing? I would only be going to a different branch of the same government that had been screwing me forever... submitting records, waiting. I was tired of it.

"Screw it," I said.

23

In July the Town's black fly control program ended and I was out of work again. A few weeks later Kathy found out she was pregnant, and I began to worry. Her due date was the end of March and we didn't have insurance. I couldn't see how the whole thing wasn't going to cost a lot of money.

We had a fair amount of money left from the sale of our house on Maui and some investments we'd made with Kathy's surplus salary, so we could pay for the baby if we had to. However, getting a job with insurance benefits made more sense.

There wasn't any work at all in Keene Valley going into the winter, so I decided to get back into flying. Insurance outweighed any concerns I had about adhesions making me sick if I flew too much. Unfortunately, there weren't any commercial helicopter operators hiring within a day's drive. I'd have to leave home to fly, which I didn't want to do. With a baby coming, Kathy did not think it would be a good idea either.

The deadline came to appeal the decision of the Board of Veterans Appeals to the Court of Veterans Appeals. Going to the Court was one more chance to hold the VA accountable, and would give me something to do through the winter. It might also raise my disability ratings and bring in a little more money, which would come in handy around March. Supporting three of us on a part-time job's salary was going to be a challenge.

I filed with the U.S. Court of Veterans Appeals in Washington, stating, "In Brief: I am representing myself. My contention is that the Veterans Administration and the Board of Veterans Appeals made numerous and serious errors in applying the facts and laws to my multiple claims before the Veterans Administration."

Within a week I got a "consent to release information" letter from the VA. They had never responded to anything as quickly as my filing with the Court, which was curious, nor had they ever asked my permission for anything before.

There wasn't much to the consent form. Most of it was a warning. The letter advised me, "In the event information to be released (to the Court of Veterans Appeals) includes information regarding drug abuse, infection with human immunodeficiency virus, alcoholism or alcohol abuse, or sickle cell anemia, I specifically consent to that disclosure as well. I understand that these records and material, and any Board of Veterans Appeals decisions will become public."

My esteem for the VA fell to an all time record low. Either they were really covering their ass for liability reasons, which was doubtful, or they were trying to intimidate me, and every other veteran applying to the Court, with the threat of exposing our personal secrets to the public.

What assholes, I thought as my anger coalesced into hatred. The Veterans Administration was actively trying to keep veterans from getting a day in court. At that point, they became my enemy, and I looked forward to proving it in the Court of Veterans Appeals.

Considering it was fall, there were absolutely no jobs in town, and a baby was due, it was a stroke of good luck when my brother-in-law bought a small excavator for his construction business and asked me if I'd like to operate it. It was a good job, but didn't last long. The machine was on metal tracks and pounded a lot. Each day my back grew worse until it ached incessantly. Even with painkillers I couldn't get comfortable at night.

That was the main reason I stopped working for Scotty, physical discomfort. But there was something else. A number of times I found myself not knowing what to do. Sometimes it wasn't even a difficult situation, but I still felt something akin to insurmountable doubt. It was odd. I couldn't remember feeling anything quite like it. Probably a lack of experience on the machine, I figured, but considered it another reason to quit.

As the months dragged on and the short dark days of winter closed in, I became more irritable. My only distraction was writing, so I threw myself headlong into it. Kathy wasn't enjoying the winter either. Even with the furnace and the wood stove going full blast we couldn't keep the place warm. Drafts flowed through the rooms like ocean currents, and it was always smoky, which raised concerns for the baby in her belly, who was becoming very visible.

By the time spring arrived it didn't take much for Kathy to talk me out of spending another winter in the house on the brook, especially with a baby. With the remainder of our savings, minus some to pay for the baby, there wasn't enough for a regular house, so we decided to build a garage with an apartment above it, a place to store our stuff and live in until we could afford something else. We drew up plans but put off beginning the project until fall, when I thought we would have more money from my summer job.

Around the time my job with the Town's black fly control program began again, I began getting correspondence from the Court of Veterans Appeals. Everything was in legalese. It didn't take long for me to realize that I was out of my league. There was a good chance I could learn my way through, but so much was at stake. I couldn't let the VA win. Besides, my job was going to keep me busy all summer, so I began looking for a lawyer.

One of the mailings from the Court stated only approved attorneys could represent veterans before them. Keith Snyder, co-author of a book Kathy had given me several years earlier, The Vietnam Veteran's Survival Guide, was listed as approved. Within the week I'd signed a pay-only-if-you-win contract with Keith, and instantly felt better.

For the first time in four years I was out of the loop. That's what it had been, a continuous cycle of hope and disappointment. After Keith took over, when I thought about the VA I basked in the knowledge that I had a real lawyer, representing me in a real court, and that's as far as I went with it.

In early April Tiger was born, and my attitude towards babies changed forever. Until that time I'd thought infants looked a lot like listless pickled monkeys, but he was beautiful, calm and gentle.

One week later, however, it was a different story. The poor little guy had colic, severe colic, of the type that required wax earplugs. Kathy bore the brunt of it, spending most of her nights with him in a rocking chair, but neither of us got much sleep for quite a while.

Before Tiger was a month old I got fired from my job with the black fly program. It was innocent enough. Thinking I could streamline the process and make the program more efficient, I broke some perfunctory rules. I didn't think what I'd done was that big of a deal so I treated the matter lightly, which offended members on the town board and cost me my job.

With fall approaching, and knowing that we had just enough money to build the garage, I hired a couple of guys and we went to work. Three months later Kathy, Tiger and I were nestled like squirrels in the attic of the new building.

In January the Court of Veterans Appeals remanded my case to the Veterans Administration, stating the VA had made serious mistakes in its handling of my claims. I thought that was good, the Court was coming down on the VA, but Keith informed me they had only listed procedural errors, that the remand was no more than a chance for the VA to restate its case.

Once again, having Keith there to interpret the Court's actions made the whole thing easy. This was nice because I had other things to worry about. We were out of money and living on the few hundred dollars a month I got from the VA, which wasn't enough.

Summer was coming and there would be seasonal jobs, but the few I'd heard about weren't paying well enough to support a family. Realistically, we weren't going to be able to make it through another winter in the Adirondacks.

"Let's go to Alaska," I suggested to Kathy one evening when we were halfway through a bottle of wine.

"Why?" she asked, surprised.

"Because we need money," I told her.

"I thought you didn't want to go back to Fairbanks," she replied, obviously entertained.

I didn't. All of my friends had left. Even Craig was in the Southeast somewhere flying Medevac for a hospital. "Not Fairbanks," I replied. "Homer."

Before we left Alaska the last time, when Kathy and I were both working and we had lots of money, she decided to spend some of it on a piece of the last frontier. We really liked Homer, so we drove down, found a nice house site on the edge of town, paid cash and forgot about it.

"I'll fly for Maritime Helicopters. We'll save up a little money, get a construction loan, and build a house on the lot we have there."

"A real house?" Kathy asked skeptically. "Not another garage?"

"I promise. A real house."

24

With our large dog, Mo, in the back seat of our little car, there was barely room for Tiger and his car seat, so our other pet, Bob The Cat, had to ride on the shelf between the back seat and the rear window. Ten days and 5,000 miles later we were in Homer. Not surprisingly, one-year-old Tiger had developed a severe aversion to being strapped in his car seat.

A few days later I began flying fulltime for Maritime. It had been over five years since I'd been in a helicopter, but it all came back in an instant. Being in the air again was wonderful, almost like the first time. The feel of the controls in my hands, the beauty of world around me, seemed new and refreshing. I really had missed it.

Tiger was Kathy's job and she took it seriously, read everything she could about babies and even took a pediatric EMT course. Her training as a scientist and knowledge of animal behavior made life a lot easier on the little guy. Instead of a helpless baby, she saw him as an immature creature trying to cope with the world around him, and she helped.

One of the more incredible things I saw her do with Tiger was communicate, getting him to respond intelligently when he was only a few weeks old. Kathy got close to him and stuck her tongue out. Almost instantly Tiger did the same. When I expressed amazement, Kathy told me, "That's the first thing they learn to do, control their tongue to breast feed. We're tongue talking."

With a steady job I qualified for a construction loan, but it wasn't as large as I'd hoped. After figuring out what the materials were going to cost, I realized we barely had enough money to hire one guy, much less a whole construction crew.

There weren't a lot of carpenters who built houses by

themselves, but I finally found a man named Tom Wood who told me that's what he liked to do.

At first I was flying nine to five, but within a few months my guts began to complain and I switched to part-time. I couldn't be sure it was related to adhesions but the fear kept me from pushing it.

As I flew less I began helping Tom more. We worked well together and always enjoyed a couple of beers at the end of the day. Unfortunately, the construction loan ran out before the house was finished and I had to let him go early.

It wasn't that bad finishing the house by myself. Only light stuff like flooring, trim, plumbing and paint were left; however, between the cold, wet, windy weather and too much lifting, my back ached constantly. Something else that was bothering me for the first time was my neck. Some days were so bad I had to twist at the waist to look sideways.

Hurting now and then was one thing, but working alone made it impossible to avoid doing things that I knew were going to make it worse. Before long I was in a lot of pain, all the time, and anger crept back into my life.

It wasn't quite the same this time around. Instead of finding fault and being critical, everything was a problem. Finishing the house had turned into a nightmare, taking twice as long as I thought it should. Mistakes were costly and frustrating.

Even Kathy became part of the problem. As often as not, whatever she did or said was an inconvenience or confrontation of some kind. A request to take out the trash frequently came across as an order, an affront, and I'd lash out. I could take a simple suggestion and turn it into a full-blown argument within seconds. I tried to catch it, walk away, but it was impossible. The difference between anger and irritation is, one peaks, the other remains maddeningly constant.

Making matters worse, with the construction loan used up and my flying only part-time, we had no money left for the house. Rather than fly more and pay someone else to finish the house, Kathy went to work for the U. S. Fish and Wildlife Service as their office manager.

Taking the job wasn't easy for her. Besides being a big step down in her career, it was tough saying goodbye to Tiger every morning. He was a beautiful child with bright blue eyes, a warm smile, and a strong attachment to his mom.

Taking care of a 14-month-old baby while building a house by myself could have been a problem, but at that age Tiger didn't crawl, he rolled. Therefore, all I had to do to keep him out of trouble was clear electrical wires, nails and that kind of stuff out of the path on which he rolled back and forth. However, before long, he began to crawl and we decided Tiger would be better off in daycare.

That was a terrible idea. Leaving Tiger everyday for work was hard on Kathy, but dropping him off at daycare was horrific for me. The sight of his little body struggling to break the grip of the lady who took him at the door, hearing him plead for me to come back and stay, ripped the heart right out of my chest.

That didn't last long, and I found other ways to keep him occupied while I finished the house. One thing I did was talk to him while I worked, so he learned a lot of profanity very early in life.

Finally, just before Christmas, the house was finished enough to move in. It was cute and comfortable with large windows that looked across Beluga Lake to the snow capped peaks of the Kenai Range. From our front porch we had uninterrupted views of three glaciers.

There was just enough flying for me not to miss it, and Kathy was doing well at her job. For all appearances life was good, but the irritation I'd been feeling affected everything I did. And my intrusive thoughts, which had all but disappeared, returned and became inexplicably intense.

I seemed to be going into a major regression. In fact, things were as bad as they'd been since we left Hawaii three years earlier. Everyone was feeling my wrath. I seemed to be apologizing constantly, feeling terrible about myself, wondering what was going on. Life was so good in every other way.

What bothered me most about the resurgence of anger was the damage it could do to Tiger. I tried to keep it from him, but we were together all the time. The outbursts were short. I always apologized and explained why I'd gotten angry. I also warned him that, under similar circumstances, it would most likely happen again.

My son was less than two years old, probably understood every other word, but he seemed to get it. Tiger weathered the storms remarkably well and, fortunately, we both found it easy to leave the episodes behind and get on with the rest of the day, usually to have quite a bit of fun.

After the house was done, Tiger and I settled into routines over the next year. We spent most of the day outside, where there was more to do and I found my anger got less traction. Every other day we went shopping. Tiger was articulate at an early age and I enjoyed interacting with him in places like stores. Other than when he disappeared.

There was nothing like stopping to read a product label, then looking up to find my son gone. As fear's strong fingers wrapped around my heart and began to squeeze, just as his name was about to burst from my throat in a roar, he'd appear, simply materialize in a spot I'd just checked. Although my temper was short, all I ever felt was relief.

We also dropped by the kid's music sessions at the school and went swimming in their pool now and then, but one thing we did every day was take a long walk. Our favorite morning adventure was through the woods on a narrow muddy trail for buttered buns and hot steamed milk at Two Sisters Bakery. From there we often went to the spit where we walked the beach, skipped stones, and looked at the stuff in the tourist shops.

Tiger and I also spent a lot of time in the marina watching the fishing boats prepare for sea. When it was stormy we sat in the restaurant at the tip of the spit, drank hot chocolate, and watched the ships fight their way through the heavy seas in and out of the bay. But our favorite place to go was the beach below Jenny Way, where we'd play on the large smooth rocks along the shore when the tide was in, and explore the sandy flats for sea creatures left behind in pools when the tide was out.

One windy winter day Tiger and I were at least a hundred yards from shore, looking at what had been left behind by a receding twenty-foot tide. When the cold gray water changed directions I didn't see or hear the silent sea flowing quickly across the sand until it was only thirty or forty feet away.

"Come on," I said, as I took Tiger's hand and headed towards the shore. In some spots the tide comes in faster than you can run.

When I looked back, the seawater had halved the distance and was about to flank us in a depression to our right. If we didn't hurry it was going to cut us off from the shore. Tiger was already running but dressed in snow pants and parka; we weren't moving fast enough. As I let go of his hand to pick him up under the arms and carry him, he fell forward into a puddle. I scooped him up and began to run, splashing through seawater up to my knees before we were finally above the tide line.

Moments later, as Tiger and I walked into Two Sisters to warm up, I noticed that the front of his jacket was frozen solid even though he'd fallen into saltwater. Surprisingly, he didn't seem to notice how wet he was, or how cold he should have been. Tiger was just happy to be getting two hot steamed milks in one day.

Kathy liked to spend time outside with her son too. Almost every evening we went for another walk with her. When winter came, and it was dark by the time she got home, we went skating on the half-mile long lake in front of our house.

It was serene on the cold black ice, gliding in the moonlight, and fun for Tiger in his sled at the end of a long rope we regularly whipped way out on the corners. Everyone loved it, even Mo, which surprised us because he had a severe case of linolephobia.

We became aware of the disorder when we moved into our house on the ranch in Hawaii. It had wood floors except for the linoleum in the kitchen. To get from the bedrooms to the rest of the house you had to go through the kitchen, which Mo did like the rest of us until the day he was going a little too fast and lost traction on the slippery surface.

For a moment the hundred and twenty pound dog froze, looking from Kathy to me, his soulful eyes pleading for help as he tried to set his nails into the impermeable material. Setting his nails only served to reduce his surface area contact and make things worse. Realizing that the situation was deteriorating, Mo made a mad dash for the living room, legs flailing in every direction. After that he couldn't cross the kitchen floor without a lot of anxiety. So it came almost as a shock when Mo followed us out on the ice to chase Tiger on his sled. Before long he got excited every time the skates came out of the closet.

As our second winter in Homer dragged on, Tiger's interests and abilities broadened and he found more ways to entertain himself. Between that and his naptime, I found time to get back to work on my book.

25

That's what I was doing, typing away at the computer, when I had my first suicidal depression. I looked up from the screen to the closed door of the bedroom closet. Whatever caught my attention had been barely noticeable. I got the impression it was a slight movement, a faint sound, nothing much, just enough to distract me from my writing.

I was sure it had come from the left, not very far away, but there wasn't anything there. Before I could think or move, a weight settled on me, pressure that quickly made breathing an effort, and an intense sadness filled my heart, a profound sense of loss and overwhelming hopelessness.

Without moving a muscle I slid slowly into a hole not much larger than myself, effortlessly descending into its confines. The containment was so complete, undeniable, even my claustrophobia didn't bother to react. I felt my senses dull. Everything around me became meaningless. Then I heard words, simple and clear, "kill yourself." I got the impression I'd been hearing them for a while, somewhere in the background as they slowly came to my attention.

It became a refrain, an unquestionable suggestion, in my head telling me to kill myself. There was no flow of adrenalin, not even an impulse to flee. I wasn't afraid. There wasn't anything to fear. It was so simple, almost gentle, but forceful.

To try to influence what was happening never occurred to me. I was powerless. I can't even say how many times I heard the refrain during the brief encounter, or at what point it became a fading echo. But in a matter of minutes the words were gone. Like a creature unexpectedly released by its captor, I sat motionless, dazed by the intensity of the experience, wondering what had just happened.

Slow to reorganize my thoughts and unexpectedly tired, I muttered, "Kill myself? What a dumb fucking idea that is."

The next time it happened, three or four days later, wasn't much different. I sank into the hole, heard the words and had no control over what was happening to me. However, the experience wasn't as disturbing because I knew I wasn't going to kill myself.

Over the years I'd read some insightful books that dealt with suicide on a variety of levels. I had thought about it philosophically, and knew people who'd taken their own lives. I was aware of the overwhelming force it could be, and that there were a limitless number of justifications for it, both irrational and rational.

Nevertheless, it seemed to me that, no matter how much one contemplated suicide, the act itself was a product of chance as much as anything, a matter of wrong time, wrong place, with no other way out.

I believed there was always another way out, some other option. I felt that all I had to do to avoid suicide was change my environment. Life was always different somewhere else, new people, new situations, and better if I picked well. I knew my views on the matter were oversimplified. But the premise, that problems can be left behind, had worked so well for me in other situations, why wouldn't it work with suicide?

After several more suicidal depressions, I began to believe they weren't any more of a threat than my intrusive thoughts. But, as they continued almost daily for weeks on end, I realized that the effects of the brief but demanding depressions were cumulative, the stress of each one building on the last. They were beginning to wear me out, similar to the effects of sleep deprivation.

When I tried to tell Kathy what was happening, the more I said the less it seemed real. A few weeks later I was having several deep depressions a day, and their saturation was broadening.

Often I was at my desk when they came along, so I wrote down some of my impressions to give them substance: "Can't seem to get rid of things bothering me. Feel threatened by everything, trembling, see movement in peripheral vision, deep inhalations, hear voices and sounds. Suicide more of an attitude, small shift, fine line."

126

I was beginning to see the actual act of suicide as something other than situational, and the effect of the sounds I heard was surprising. I'd had ringing in my ears since I got shot down the last time, and learned to live with it, but the sounds I heard after the depressions began were different.

Although faint and meaningless they were enough like voices, or music, to repeatedly catch my attention. I couldn't stop myself from trying to make sense of them; and, the constant distractions became a noticeable drain of my energy and mental functions.

While I was dealing with suicidal depressions and fatigue, Tiger was becoming a person, a very attractive child. He had a way of looking at me and smiling that just made me feel good. Mothers in the market left their children to comment on his even disposition and incredible eyes, a blue that reflected the mood of whatever surrounded him. When he spoke, his thoughts were organized and words well chosen. Tiger was sunlight and music, while I, by comparison, was not.

It was definitely a Beauty and the Beast situation. My mind was under a lot of pressure and I couldn't stop venting. I spent a lot of time apologizing, and took every opportunity I could to make it clear that it wasn't his fault, that it was my problem and I was doing my best to deal with it.

Most three-year-olds would have withdrawn, not had anything to do with me. But Tiger patiently deflected the blunt force of my indiscriminate anger, let it go by, and then got back to what he liked most, having fun. He certainly helped keep my heart and head in the right place.

Living with my anger and mood swings was one thing, as was putting up with intrusive thoughts, but the suicidal depressions were different. Along with wearing me down, they were eroding my will, confusing me. I didn't want to talk to Kathy about it. She didn't need the extra burden. But I had to talk to someone, so I turned to the Veterans Administration, not claims, just the medical department.

26

The VA Regional Hospital was in Anchorage. That's where I had to go to see their psychiatrist. It was a long drive, but I began to look forward to it.

I left Homer at three in the morning. Getting up that early wasn't easy, but worth it because no one else was on the road. The little Audi we drove from New York was getting old, but was still light and quick. In a couple of hours I was in the Kenai Mountains where, at that time of year, there was always black ice.

I never knew where the ice was until I felt that certain looseness in the steering wheel. As long as I didn't put on the brakes, or even let up on the gas too fast, I was okay. The all-wheel drive of that 5000 Quattro was perfectly balanced. All I had to do was tell myself to relax, and slowly let up on the gas until the car began to drift, then get back on it a bit, back off again, etc., until I had it slowed down. Four hours after leaving Homer I'd roll into Anchorage feeling pretty good. Rick Sword had been right... hanging it out is a good stress reliever.

The VA psychiatrist was a decent guy but, once again, wanted to put me in an inpatient PTSD program, commit me. Before too long he turned me over to their clinic in Kenai, a one-man operation that was a lot closer to home.

The doctor in Kenai became increasingly uncomfortable when we began talking about my suicidal depressions. After a few visits he admitted he was more of a counselor and not really equipped for this kind of thing. In turn, he set me up with a private psychologist in town, Kathleen Dinius, who readily admitted that she didn't know anything about PTSD but was interested in working with me. For my part, I knew I was running out of options.

Kathleen listened to my story and suggested lithium carbonate, a well-known treatment for bipolar disorder. I declined. Over the years the psychiatrists at the VA had given me a variety of drugs, and they hadn't worked at all. In fact, most of them seemed to make things worse. The last one I'd tried left me lying on the floor holding onto the knowledge that its effects would wear off in a few hours.

She told me lithium was different, a naturally occurring salt used in making glass and ceramics, and that it often worked for people who react adversely to other manic-depressive drugs. So I gave it a try.

Kathleen told me it would be weeks before it took affect, but I noticed subtle changes in days. By the end of the week I was less anxious, less irritable, and my depressions weren't anywhere near as tiring. However, my flight surgeon told me I couldn't take lithium and fly, so I had to stop working for Maritime. That didn't bother me a lot. They usually called me in on holidays and in wicked weather, when no one else wanted to fly. Besides, with Kathy working full-time we didn't need the money as much.

The lithium made a noticeable difference. It didn't eliminate my suicidal depressions by any means, but their frequency and severity decreased. From then on, instead of sinking into a hole and listening to my brain tell me to kill myself I simply got depressed. It was the first time I felt as if I had any control over my suicidal depressions at all.

As usual, as one thing got better, something else got worse. As spring approached, it was my back. One cold rainy day followed another in a constant transition from freeze to thaw, right through May. The low temperature and high humidity kept me in constant pain. Before long I was taking record amounts of Darvocet.

When a warning came from the Veterans Administration that the painkiller could cause liver damage, and I realized how difficult it would be to live without the drug, I considered surgery. But the orthopedic surgeon at the VA Hospital in Anchorage was skeptical.

After a brief interview and examination he told me, "You're not in enough pain for surgery." However, he ordered a CT scan, the first one I'd had. After taking a look at the CT scan report he changed his mind. "Lateral disc herniation on the right at L3-4, impinging the right L3 nerve root lateral to the neural foramen," it read in part.

"We can operate on that," the doctor told me, pointing to a spot on the CT scan that was clipped to the viewing screen.

The detail in the image was amazing. I could see exactly what he was talking about. There was a polyp. It looked like a little balloon about the size of his fingertip, and it was oozing from between two vertebrae. It reminded me of a burst dam, the way it spread out in a fan. Then he pointed out the nerve that was pinned against a piece of bone.

"But there's a fifty-fifty chance surgery will make things worse," he said. "So, if you can live with the discomfort it's causing you now, you probably should. If it gets worse, you can always come back."

"Thanks," I replied. "That's probably good advice."

Although the ruptured disc and pinched nerve looked bad, and were causing me pain, it was intermittent. The orthopedic surgeon told me that if things didn't go well in surgery, the pain might become permanent. It wasn't worth the risk, I decided. Plus, although it had been nearly five years since they'd opened me up and cut my adhesions, I hadn't forgotten how much I disliked being operated on.

Even though I was unconscious at the time, the procedure left several indelible impressions. One was the distinct feeling of a scalpel slicing flesh. The other was the ghostlike imprints left by the surgeon's fingers on the organs he touched.

The summer passed quickly with Kathy working nine to five and my balancing my time between Tiger, writing, and psychological disorders. In the fall, my attorney wrote to say my case with the U.S. Court of Veterans Appeals was in the hands of the judge. About the same time I finished my book, Easy Target: The Long Strange Trip of a Scout Pilot in Vietnam. I was all set to send it to potential publishers, until I talked to Kathy.

"It's not ready," she said when I told her what I was thinking.

"I'm sure it could use another rewrite, but I think it's good enough for someone to take a look at," I responded.

"Not until you write the English language version; figure

130

out where commas go, what a run-on sentence is, and how to stay in one tense," she told me. Kathy was right. I didn't know how to punctuate, or a lot about grammar in general. "Maybe they have some courses you can take at the college," she suggested. Homer had a small community college, and they did have courses in grammar, so I wisely took her advice.

At that point life was good again. I was learning a lot in school and enjoying the company of the young students. My case against the Veterans Administration was before the judge, and the lithium seemed to be holding its own against my suicidal depressions. That's why it came as a surprise when I caught a glimpse of what appeared to be the end of my life.

The lithium was doing what it was supposed to do, limiting the bipolar mood swings, but it was also covering up a problem. The leveling effect of the drug was masking my mental fatigue.

Although I no longer felt the depressions as much, they were still there, taking a little more out of me each day, wearing me down. Everything seemed to be okay, but my mind was exhausted. That's what I saw as the end of my life... sleep. Suicide finally had some appeal. I could see the peaceful side.

As Christmas drew near I took stock of my situation. For the first time I genuinely thought an untimely demise might be in my future. Not soon, but getting closer. Like any tired person, I felt I couldn't defend myself forever. I had to tell Kathy.

"Are you worried?" she asked after I told her what I was feeling.

"Not really," I said, not wanting to make it sound any worse. "I don't think anything's going to happen. But I'm amazed at how screwed up I am, and thought you should know."

I also told Kathleen. I'd been working with the psychologist for six months. Although we had gotten into ruts of sort, and weren't making a lot progress, she was intelligent and I didn't feel like going through it all over again with someone else.

"To be honest, Kathleen," I said one day. "I still can't unequivocally say I have PTSD. I can see the incidents, what is happening, but I just can't relate. Maybe I have mental blocks. Anyway, I'm tired of it."

"What is it you're trying to say?" she asked.

"I've been trying to deal with this shit for five or six years,"

I told her. "And I still don't have any idea what's going on." I looked at her, exasperated. But she just stared back. It was obviously up to me. "I'm afraid it's time for a silver bullet."

"A what?" Kathleen asked.

"You know... a silver bullet. The only thing that can kill the beast, either a vampire or werewolf, I can't remember which." I paused, trying to figure out exactly what I was saying. "But in this case it would have to be more like a model," I explained, feeling good about the idea. "If you can give me some kind of framework, even an overview of the mess I'm in, I might stand a chance of working my way out of it."

"Well, PTSD is..."

"Not the VA version, or the AMA," I interrupted. "I know them. I'm talking about something else... some similar experience that relates."

She thought for a moment. "All I can draw from my experience has to do with women who've been raped. Society can't prepare them for the trauma they are exposed to. Which is very much, I believe, like men in combat. To make matters worse, both you and rape victims have to deal with an unsympathetic, if not openly hostile, society unwilling to let you back in." Then she added, "But there is no model or framework, per se. As far as working yourself out of PTSD, as I understand it, the prognosis is not so much a cure, as a matter of learning to live with it."

Right time, right place, or simply well put on both our parts, it didn't take long to benefit from Kathleen's analogy. The relationship between the brutality of rape and the shock of combat somehow connected. I also saw for the first time that, like so many people before me, whether they were a combat veteran or rape victim, I was just going to have to learn to live with it.

27

Literally the day after Christmas I got a letter from Keith, my attorney. My case before the US Court of Veterans Appeals in Washington was on hold.

The Veterans Administration had won a lawsuit against the Court of Veterans Appeals and, based on a technicality, a number of cases currently before the Court might be eliminated. He said mine was one of them, concluding, "It could mean that you lose everything and the Court will dismiss the case as untimely."

After all the years of trying to work with the Veterans Administration, the frustration and humiliation, then the chance to challenge them on a level playing field comes along, only to have them hide behind a frivolous technicality. What assholes, I thought once again. The VA was fighting, by any means possible, the veterans they were charged with helping... unbelievable. The anger rose quickly, and dropped off. I'm becoming immune to their tactics, I thought without satisfaction.

In the same letter Keith suggested I open a new claim with the Veterans Administration in Anchorage. He believed the VA was wrong in their "finding of facts" and that my case, if dismissed on a technicality, still had merit.

Opening another claim just seemed like asking for more of a bad thing to me, and for what? To expose myself, and my family, to more frustration and anger so I could end up fighting them in court seven years later?

Getting satisfaction, even dental coverage, hardly seemed worth it in light of the Veterans Administration's incredible tenacity. However, Keith was the lawyer, and I certainly knew the process.

Several weeks later I submitted a new claim to the VA in

Anchorage, who responded by asking for records "since your discharge from service." They even asked for a certified copy of our marriage certificate. I had to laugh, and then went about photocopying records in my file and sending them in.

Around the same time Kathy mentioned that a position with her office was opening on Adak, a tiny and sparsely populated island more than a thousand miles southwest of Homer in the Aleutian Islands. If Homer's weather was bad, in the Aleutians it was horrific.

The thin chain of 300 small volcanic islands stretches 1,200 miles between Alaska and Russia, the frigid Bering Sea to the north and the warmer Pacific Ocean to the south. Along the island chain, where warm and cold water meet, the climate becomes unstable. Gale force winds, freezing rain and zero visibility are the norm. Adak, almost halfway to Russia, not only had the worst weather, it was an active volcano with small earthquakes daily and frequent "window rattlers."

Kathy was interested in the job because she'd go from Fish and Wildlife's office manager in Homer to their wildlife biologist for Adak and the surrounding islands. However, it wasn't as easy to explain why I wanted to go to the remote, desolate island. I told Kathy it was for the ocean kayaking, to experience something new, but that was a small part of it.

When Kathy told me about the job, where it was didn't matter. I had to go. When we left Alaska for Hawaii it was for a change. I thought I'd burned out. And when we moved from Hawaii to New York it was to settle down. We moved back to Alaska again for work. When Kathy suggested leaving Homer for Adak, I didn't need a reason and knew why. I was running again, trying to leave my problems behind, and that was exactly what I wanted to do.

Unfortunately, only weeks after Kathy applied for the job, the Navy base on the island began downsizing. Fish and Wildlife announced that applicants for the biologist position couldn't bring families because medical services weren't going to be available for dependents.

I was disappointed; however, with the opportunity no longer there, I wondered what the hell I'd been thinking. I would have been miserable in the damp cold of the Aleutian Islands. My back would have driven me crazy.

I didn't want to go to Adak anymore, but I still wanted to leave. It wasn't something I thought about all the time, but when I did I felt desperate. A little while later, when Kathy told me there was another job opening with Fish and Wildlife that she was interested in, I didn't hesitate to ask where.

"On Maui," she said.

"You're kidding," I laughed, thinking how ironic fleeing to Maui would be.

"Seriously," she told me. "They're looking for a refuge manager."

"A refuge manager?" Kathy had a Master's degree in wildlife biology and a lot of experience with the Forest Service, but only two years with Fish and Wildlife as an office manager... quite a leap to refuge manager. "That would really be a big step forward in your career," I mused.

"You wouldn't mind going back?" Kathy asked.

"Adak," I told her. "Maui. They're both islands."

"Office manager, refuge manager," she laughed. "They're both managers."

Meanwhile the Veterans Administration in Anchorage kept asking for records and reports, which I sent reflexively. It was pretty much the same stuff I submitted in Hawaii. The only change I needed to make was on form 21-8940, my Employment History. I was up to twelve employers in eight years.

Spring came slowly, but with the warmer weather Tiger and I got outside for longer periods of time, and I began to feel better, more energetic. The depressions became less and less frequent and my mood swings more controllable.

The warmer weather was good for my back too. The pain almost disappeared, as did the pressing need to leave Homer, but two months later Kathy got the refuge manager job on Maui.

While we were packing up the contents of our house I got another letter from Keith, along with a copy of a rating decision from the VA's Adjudication Board in Anchorage. They were responding to the claim Keith had me open six months earlier.

In their decision, the Veterans Administration in Anchorage service connected the thoracic part of my spine even though I hadn't put in a claim for that part of my back. Evidently the last

CT scan showed some deteriorating discs closer to my head, along with the herniated disc pinching a nerve lower in my spine.

They raised the total rating for my back to 60%, and my rating for PTSD to 50%. They were being really nice, I thought. Then I read, "compensation at the 100% rate is granted." They'd granted 100% before, while I was in the Lahey Clinic for surgery, four or five days altogether, so I had to look at it twice. There was no mistake. They had rated me 100% disabled due to unemployability.

For a moment I was speechless. Compensation at the rate of a hundred percent, 750 dollars a month, would pay most of our fixed expenses. Financial concerns, as we'd know them over the last few years, were gone. Then, as I read on, I knew it was finally over. The Adjudication Board in Anchorage had also given me dental coverage for my entire mouth. I wouldn't have to worry about any major medical condition for the rest of my life. I was done.

The only flaw in an otherwise incredible turn of events was, in the back of my mind I knew that my victory was tenuous at best. Given the attitude and impunity the VA had demonstrated so often, it was entirely possible they might simply decide to take it all away. They'd shown their disrespect for the rules more than once. So I never really put it behind me until the Court of Veterans Appeals weighed in with its decision in my case.

Although the Veterans Administration's lawsuit before the United States Court of Veterans Appeals managed to get half of my claims dropped on technicalities, the judge ruled on what was left.

He threw out every one of the VA's rating decisions dating back fifteen years, and wrote, "Although presented with a substantial amount of evidence supporting each of the veteran's claims, the Board failed to provide even a single reason why the negative evidence outweighed the positive."

His words meant more to me than dental coverage. It totally validated my near-obsessive belief that the VA claims process had not been fair. However, what really made it work for me was the finality of the Court's ruling. Even the highest authority in the Veterans Administration couldn't change the decision of a Federal Court.

PANIC ATTACKS

Panic attacks really did not become an issue until months after Tiger, Kathy and I left Homer and moved back to Maui. However, many years earlier, before I knew anything about PTSD, something happened that was unforgettable. I've included this event because the signs of panic attacks can be misinterpreted. Often, although abnormal, the symptoms don't seem out of place.

I believe my first major panic attack happened in Singapore almost six months after I left Darcie and Zach in California for a job in Indonesia. I was waiting for my visa to be renewed so I could get back to Borneo. For the last six months I'd been resupplying a seismic crew working on the large island in the South China Sea.

The mostly native crew was laying strings of geophones and dynamite charges along trails they hacked through the dense jungle. When the charges were sequentially detonated, the sensors picked up the return shock waves. With the recorded data, geologists in the home office could identify potential oil-bearing geological formations.

Most of my days consisted of flying between the dirt airstrip in Muarateweh, where airplanes brought in supplies, and holes cut in the jungle by the seismic crew. It was a lot of work to cut down trees that grew up to 200 feet tall, so the men didn't make the holes any bigger than they had to, usually just wide enough to accommodate my rotor blades.

Typically I'd take off with 300 pounds of dynamite slung underneath the helicopter on a fifty-foot line. In the passenger compartment behind me there was usually a fifty-five gallon drum of high-octane gasoline for the generators, along with bags of fish and rice to feed the crew. The blasting caps went on the copilot's seat beside me.

I'd been warned that it was unwise to put volatile substances near each other in hot, humid weather, especially the fuel and the dynamite.

When I got to where the crew was I'd come to a hover about 100 feet above the tops of the trees and begin an uncontrolled descent towards the crude helipad among the tangle of cut limbs on the jungle floor below.

The helicopter was always so overloaded it simply couldn't develop enough lift to hold me at a hover that high in the air, so the descent was fairly rapid until the dynamite in the sling under the helicopter hit the ground. Then the aircraft got a lot lighter and I'd get some lift out of the rotor blades. But I only had fifty feet in which to slow down or I'd crash on top of the dynamite. Going into the holes was one of those things that always felt like it wasn't going to work, but I got use to it.

What I did was demanding but repetitious; fortunately, there was always the odd job for a break. One of the more memorable ones came from the representative of a British exploration company who showed up at our base hangar in Balikpapan one afternoon while I was in from the field for routine maintenance. I'd just landed and was on my way out the door for a cold beer, but had to talk to him because I was the only one in the hangar who spoke his language.

The Englishman told me in his crisp way that one of his team members, a mineralogist traveling by canoe, was dying in the jungle west of where I was working. He said his friend was unable to get out by river because of heavy rains and impassable rapids.

"You're the only one around here who has any idea of the lay of the land out there," he told me. "And we were wondering if you'd be good enough to go after him."

I asked him to show me where the guy was. "Certainly," he said, pulling a folded map out of his briefcase. He opened it on a table and pointed to a spot marked with an X. The map was of the entire island of Borneo, and the place he put his finger on was in the middle of an expanse of white paper. He wanted me to go to a place that wasn't on the map!

"I don't think I can do it," I told him. "There aren't enough landmarks to find him."

"Yes," he agreed. "Mapping hasn't been completed yet. However," he added quickly. "This river," he pointed to a thin blue line in the field of white, "leads right to the spot. His man will light a fire at the appointed time so you'll be able to pinpoint his position. We have good radio contact."

When I gave the map a closer look, I realized the spot he had marked was at least a hundred miles past any point I'd been to, and well beyond the fuel range of my helicopter. "Still can't do it," I told him.

After I explained why, he asked, "Well, what kind of helicopter has the range?"

I told him I wasn't sure, but there were two other companies in Balikpapan and he should talk to them. That evening he was at our hanger telling me that neither of the other companies was willing to take on the mission. "They referred me back to you, I'm afraid," he explained. "They said their aircraft don't have the range to get there from here. That your base in Muarateweh is the closest to him." For a second time I told him the guy was out of my range too. "Well then," he sighed. "I guess he's a dead man." I looked to see if he was joking. From all appearances he wasn't.

"You could carry extra fuel," I said speculatively. "Like the fifty gallon drums we put in the back for the seismic crews. Just fill it with jet fuel."

"Would it be enough to make the trip?" he asked, as interested as a proper Brit could be.

I looked at the map again. "Probably. If you don't have to make too many turns and the weather is good."

He beamed at me, "Then you'll do it?"

"What? No," I told him. "That's just how it could be done." Several minutes later, after some serious flattery and the promise of a case of good wine, French, not British, I agreed to give it a try.

When the company I worked for approved the use of its helicopter for the mission, I was told that, in the event I had an engine failure or ran out of fuel, I shouldn't wait around to be rescued, but should find my own way home. The triple canopy jungle was so dense they weren't even going to look for me.

The next day I was in the general area of the spot marked on the map. There was no sign of smoke, or the mineralogist I was looking for. The reserve fuel was in the tank and my fuel gauge indicated I was at the point of no return. As I made my turn to head home I saw a thin column of smoke hanging above the jungle canopy far up a side valley. God damn it, I said to myself.

Anxious minutes later I landed in a clearing beside a stream, and immediately shut down to conserve fuel. As the rotor blades stopped turning, a native ran up and, unbelievably, handed me a Coca Cola.

While I was wondering how the bottled beverage had made its way to the middle of Borneo, the young man who brought it to me pointed towards the stream, and said, "He come. Clean now." Knee deep in the water was a naked white man, my dying passenger, lathering up to look good in town.

When we landed at Balikpapan, the Brits didn't seem to notice that their man wasn't sick, which left me feeling a little used. Fortunately, they made good on the promised case of French wine, which was excellent, so it was worth it. Life was interesting, an exotic adventure, and there was no reason to suspect I was about to have my first panic attack, particularly while I was on vacation.

We worked a three-week on, one-week off, schedule. Usually I spent my time off in Singapore or Bali. I loved the island of Bali, its gentle people and unspoiled natural beauty, but also enjoyed the metropolis of Singapore for its fine food and interesting mix of cultures.

I always stayed at the Raffles Hotel, which, along with the Cricket Club and St. Andrews Cathedral, comprised the colonial heart of the city. Above the main bar in the Raffles there was a picture of the Queen, and above one of the urinals in the men's bathroom was the inscription, "Somerset Maugham Pissed Here".

In the bar one night I met two Germans. They were an odd couple. The older man was tall and distinguished, the younger one, stocky and disgruntled. They weren't the type of people I ordinarily befriended. I don't even remember why we began talking, but the older man bought me a drink and we began trading expatriate stories. On parting, he asked me to join them the next day at the Turf Club for the races.

I lost every bet until my host informed me, "In Singapore, you do not use statistics to pick the winner. Before the race you look at the horses when they are available for viewing. And then place your bet on the one that looks drugged the least." A moment later he added, with a knowing nod, "The Chinese."

The next night I ran into my German friends in the bar again. After a few drinks the older man made a surprising offer. If I'd fly under the cover of darkness to a designated spot 80 miles off the coast, they'd be waiting for me in the water with hundreds of pounds of diamonds. He told me the uncut gems had gone down with a German U-Boat, and that they would pay me well for my time and expertise.

My initial reaction was to laugh and say no. It was too much, not to mention illegal, which they said it wasn't. But I'd had a few drinks and entertained the idea for the rest of the evening; mostly for the sake of conversation and the alcohol the old man kept buying.

The next morning I thought I'd be lucky to survive my hangover, much less a landing at night in the open ocean. In anything but perfect conditions it would be suicide. At some point one of them had also mentioned that the helicopter was going to be stolen. The whole thing was ridiculous.

I was still suffering when I sat down that evening with the Germans and told them I wouldn't be able to pick them up at sea. The older man asked why, and I told him about the difficulties in water landings and the unforeseeable problems with stolen helicopters. When I was finished the younger man glanced at his partner as if to say, I told you so. Then he glared at me.

That night there was a knock on my room door. I opened it and, without a word, the younger German pushed me out of the way, came in and locked the door. Then he went straight to the phone by my bed and ripped the cord out of the wall.

He pointed to a chair. "Sit down!" he ordered in a malicious tone. All the while he never took his eyes off mine. I believed that he was a very dangerous person. "You know what we are planning." He paused for a second. "There are people here who would like someone like yourself to tell them about it."

"Look," I began uncertainly. "To me it was just a wild idea you guys had. For all I know you were joking. I mean, I told you it wasn't something you could do, land at night..."

"That doesn't matter," he said.

"Maybe, but I really don't have a lot of information, and

there's no reason for me to..."

"Why shouldn't I get rid of you?" he asked. "That would be easier than worrying about it."

"No," I told him, horrified, having a hard time comprehending what he was saying. "There's really no reason to worry." My voice cracked and began to waver. "I have absolutely no reas..."

"I don't know that," he growled, cutting me off for the third time. Then he told me that it was up to him whether I would live, and I crumbled. I could feel the soft trickle of tears on my cheeks. "Look, please don't kill me," I begged. "There just isn't any reason. It's not necessary, I swear to you." He stared at me for a very long moment, then got up, unlocked the door and left.

I bolted the door behind him and stood there trembling uncontrollably, wondering if I should climb out a window in case he changed his mind and came back. Instead I sat down. My room was on the third floor.

A few minutes later, when I'd calmed down and felt certain the German wasn't coming back, I had to ask myself if he'd been serious. Was he really going to kill me, or just trying to scare me enough to keep me quiet?

29

Everything about that night in Singapore was bizarre. The Germans' ridiculous plan and the threat on my life were unbelievable, and breaking down in tears was unforgivable. In my mind there was ample reason to be frightened, even to plea for my life, but not to lose control of myself.

At the time I was extremely embarrassed, thought the tears were a sign of weakness, possibly cowardice. Later I came to believe my reaction had as much to do with panic attacks as fear for my life.

The immediate and total loss of control, the inability to think past the threat, or think at all for that matter, was too much like subsequent attacks. Also, I've never experienced anything like it anywhere else; even in situations more life threatening, like the evening in Vietnam several months before I got shot down for the last time.

My door gunner and I were cruising low-level over a large expanse of defoliated jungle and flew right through a helicopter trap, three heavy machine guns set up in a triangle a hundred meters apart. They were well hidden in the quick regrowth of the understory, while the leafless trees kept us exposed to their fire with no place to take cover.

If we hadn't been flying straight into the setting sun, my door gunner and I might have seen some clues. But we were relaxed, completely unprepared; the day was almost over.

If my wingman hadn't been a new guy who didn't know how to put down effective cover fire, and if I weren't tired, things might have gone differently too. But we'd been flying since sunup and it had been over 100 degrees all day.

When our helicopter was in the middle of the trap, the

machine guns began shooting simultaneously. Bullets hit the engine before I moved the controls. It was the first time I'd had my engine shot out, so I was pretty surprised but knew what to do.

For a year our instructor pilots had drilled it into us, "Bottom the collective the instant you lose your engine. You have only seconds before you also lose rotor rpm." They chopped the throttle on us all the time, usually while we were distracted, until taking the lift out of the rotor system became a conditioned reflex.

However, I couldn't lower the collective. There were trees all around us. Large sun-bleached limbs reached out in every direction. If we hit them our rotor blades would break off and we'd fall to the ground out of control. So I held the collective up, searching, even when the low rotor rpm horn began to blare in my ears, indicating the main rotor blades were turning below a safe speed. I knew that our time in the air was limited to a matter of seconds. Then more bullets hit.

There was a muffled explosion and the stricken helicopter shuddered as the volatile fumes in the fuel tank ignited. A fraction of a second later my peripheral vision caught something coming over the bulkhead to my left... Fire! Reflexively I closed my eyes as the burning gases enveloped me.

The smell of scorched hair filled my nostrils when my mustache cooked to a crisp. There was also a strange feeling in my mouth, a slight pressure, which I later realized was fire consuming oxygen and expanding. At the same time there was a searing pain in the back of my neck where the nylon nape-strap of my flight helmet melted into my skin.

Before the fuel tank exploded, I didn't want to go into the trees. With the helicopter on fire, we couldn't. If the machine hit anything solid the ruptured fuel cell would send jet fuel everywhere, turning us into a fireball. A fair number of scouts burned when they crashed. The ones who lived through it were going to spend the rest of their lives dealing with skin grafts and pain.

A quick look at my instruments showed the main rotor speed well below the bottom of the green. According to the manufacture's specifications the helicopter could no longer perform a successful forced landing. But I fought the need to put the collective down, frantically scanning the labyrinth of limbs in front of me for an opening of any kind.

Instinctively I tightened my grip on the controls and pulled back into the questionable security of my armored seat, trying to distance myself from what I knew was going to happen next, a very violent trip to the ground below.

There was a spot directly in front of us, a little depression about a hundred feet away. There were a few trees, but that's where I was going to zero the airspeed, put down the collective, and use our remaining rotor rpm to chop through the dead limbs. Then, just above that spot, there was a silver flash. It didn't mean anything to me, but it was too bright to miss. When it flashed again in the same place I realized that it was sunlight reflecting off water, not far away, and I knew what I had to do.

First I had to get over the trees between the water and us. With no engine and the rotor rpm so low, pulling up on the collective for more lift wasn't going to help. That would slow the rotor blades down even more quickly. The only thing I had left was some precious airspeed.

As we began to settle into the tops of the trees I slowly brought the cyclic back. That was the most control I've ever exercised in the cockpit, slowing the aircraft down while we were on fire and about to fall out of the sky, while trying to get to a landing spot still hundreds of feet in front of us.

Our altitude held, but a quick glance at the instruments showed us dropping through 40 mph. Somewhere between 20 and 30 we were going to fall out of the air no matter what I did. The rotor blades above me were turning so slowly I could see them individually as they went by. It was insane.

We cleared the trees by a few feet. With the remaining inertia I nosed the helicopter over, hoping to regain enough speed to do a successful running landing. There wasn't a chance of doing a normal landing. Just before we hit the water, I told my door gunner to jump.

He had climbed out of the helicopter when it exploded and was standing beside me on the landing gear, clinging to the doorframe above my head. A raging fire was burning where his seat had been.

As the landing gear slipped below the surface of the water, I rolled the aircraft to the left. When it came to a stop the fuselage began to settle. Not wanting to go down with the ship, I undid my seatbelt and scrambled for the open door. But the cyclic, which was thrashing around because the broken rotor blades were deflecting off the water, caught my leg and pulled me back into the cockpit, inadvertently saving my life. If I'd made it out the door the rotor blades would have killed me.

That was it, the last straw as it were, and I slumped back in my seat, completely overwhelmed by the ordeal. However, as the water crept over my feet, fear got me moving again.

By then the blades had stopped turning so I crawled out of the cockpit without incident, stood on a piece of landing gear protruding from the water, did a little dive to clear the wreckage, and went straight to the bottom of the pond.

My metal chest protector, thirty-six pounds of fiberglass and steel, dragged me down like an anchor. I knew I had to get to the surface and instinctively began a vigorous dog paddle, but soon realized I wasn't going anywhere.

Getting shot up, the explosion, the desperate search for a place to put the helicopter down, had taken their toll. I was disoriented, confused and beginning to run out of oxygen. My arms were getting heavy, moving more slowly, thoughts were beginning to drift. I was barely aware of time but knew it was running out. I couldn't think of anything else to do but swim. For the third or fourth time in as many minutes I felt panic begin to rise, but even that was half-hearted by then.

The next thing I remember thinking was, "So this is it," and knew I was very close to taking a breath of water. Then I stood up... didn't think about it, just got to my feet. The water was around four feet deep.

After living through something like getting shot down on fire over trees, and not losing control, there was little doubt in my mind that breaking into tears that night in the Raffles Hotel was an abnormal reaction, even for the situation.

I also believed it was an isolated incident until shortly after Tiger was born. Then something happened that was almost as disconcerting.

Around two in the morning I came out of a sound winter sleep, something I didn't do without reason. At first it wasn't obvious what woke me, but then I heard what sounded like the distant drone of an airplane's engines. I closed my eyes but couldn't get back to sleep. The noise was getting louder, or closer, I couldn't tell which. When I sat up it sounded like the noise was actually coming from within the walls. It was still growing louder, distracting, quickly becoming a source of irritation.

I shook Kathy. "Do you hear a humming sound?" I asked as soon as she showed signs of life. She'd gotten less than eight cumulative hours of sleep in the last three days because Tiger had been having a rough time.

Kathy barely opened her eyes, and said, "No."

"I thought it was a plane, but now it's coming from the walls," I explained. "It sounds sort of electrical."

Kathy frowned. "Don't wake the baby."

"Okay," I replied, trying to relax. "I'm going downstairs to throw the main breaker. If it stops I'll know it's an electrical problem."

The humming stopped halfway down the stairs, but I opened the circuit breaker anyway. Moments later I was back in bed and the humming returned as loud as ever. I threw the quilt back and almost jumped out of bed. I had to get away from it.

Kathy woke up. "What's happening?" she asked, reasonably irritated.

"I know you don't hear it," I began, confused and anxious. "But I'm hearing a deep humming noise. It's probably in my head." Then I realized that the noise disappeared while I was talking. "I'm going to watch some TV," I told her. "Sorry for waking you. Go back to sleep."

My neck was stiff when I woke up in a chair the next morning, but it was worth it. The humming sound was gone, which was good because it would have driven me insane in no time. I couldn't imagine where the sound had come from, but hoped it would never return.

Six years later, when panic attacks became an issue, they reminded me of my reaction to the humming sound in the walls and the incident in the Raffles Hotel. The way they came on suddenly, completely overwhelmed me and left almost as quickly.

30

When Tiger, Kathy and I got to Maui, similar to the other times we'd moved, there was a welcome reprieve from my problems. Things had been fine the last few months in Homer, but in the warmth of the tropical sun my back issues basically disappeared. Before long I quit taking lithium because I couldn't remember when I'd had my last suicidal depression. Even my temper wasn't as bad.

I still got upset and would lose it, but daily, not hourly. There were also patterns. My anger had become almost predictable, which made it a little easier to live with. It also seemed awkward and out of place in my new environment. Tiger was four and needed more socialization, so most mornings we hung out with playgroups in the community centers.

I already stood out in that setting. At the time it was unusual for a man to be the primary caregiver. The moms were nice, but didn't trust me. I had to earn their respect, prove I was a good mom, which wasn't difficult. I'd been taking care of my son for three years and could rock a kid on my hip as well as any of them. Nevertheless, they were wary. Any sign of a temper would have made me an instant pariah and cost Tiger friends, which helped keep my anger in check.

Things got easier the next year. Tiger began preschool and I had four more hours a day than I'd had in the last four years. He was also old enough to swim in the ocean. Every day after school we went directly to the beach for a couple of hours. Having been conditioned to stay out of Alaska's deadly waters, it took some convincing to get him into the ocean the first time, but once in, he was like a fish.

Spending the afternoons at the beach with my son became

the high point of the day. We bodysurfed the smaller waves, getting rides of 30 or 40 feet without a problem, built sand castles, took walks, dove into the waves and let them roll us around on the beach like driftwood.

Quite often, when we were in the ocean close together, the sunlight reflecting off the water caught in Tiger's eyes. The clear blue light they radiated was literally stunning.

Kathy's life was going well too. Her rapid rise through the hierarchy of the U.S. Fish and Wildlife Service brought out the best in her. She was a considerate person with a technical education. The combination was proving to be an efficient and effective refuge manager. The only problem I had with her work was how much time she spent doing it, ten hours a day, six days a week.

Kealia Pond, the shallow wetland in the middle of the new refuge, was home to everything from migratory ducks to endangered Hawaiian stilts and coots. There was a mile of beach on the ocean side of the refuge where an endangered species of Hawaiian sea turtle, the hawksbill, occasionally nested in the sand above high tide.

Unfortunately, the beach was also home to dirt bikers and four wheelers. The sand dunes had been their playground for years. At night the beach had other uses, including drug sales. Several people had warned Kathy that there would be trouble if she tried to change things.

It was a mess, but Kathy handled it well. She was persuasive without being adversarial. She was also fortunate to have Larry, a mellow Hawaiian and veteran of the Maui Police Force, as the refuge law enforcement officer. Within months the four wheelers and dirt bikers were gone, as was the nightly drug traffic on the beach, and Kathy had begun work on a boardwalk that would give people access to the refuge while protecting the sand dunes and turtle nesting areas.

As hoped, with the off-road vehicles gone, there were increased signs of sea turtle use of the beach, including more successful nesting. Then the media got in on it. Bringing back an endangered species made good press.

Soon, everyone on the island knew what Kathy was doing for Maui. She particularly appreciated the sentiments of Native

Hawaiians who often told her how much they appreciated her care for the a'ina, the land.

We also got to meet an astronaut through Kathy's job. Chuck Brady had been on mission STS-78 aboard the space shuttle Columbia. He was visiting the island and met Kathy at the refuge.

A few days later we went to dinner with him. Chuck told us that he made a point of visiting refuges and other sanctuaries wherever he traveled. He went on to say that, after being in space, like most of his fellow astronauts, he had developed an intense appreciation for the natural state of our incredible blue-green orb suspended in infinite darkness.

The first year back on Maui was good to all three of us. Life was decidedly better. I even thought it might stay that way, but no such luck. Once again, as one thing improved something else got worse.

About the time Tiger went to preschool I noticed that being among people was different than it had been in the past. I've never liked crowds, could even be labeled a recluse at times, but being around people didn't usually upset me. However, being surrounded by them, even a crowded store, began to make me uncomfortable. It was almost like fear. I could feel the adrenalin in my blood and the tension in my muscles. Then one day I got up and walked out of a movie before it began.

As the lights high in theater's ceiling dimmed, I slid effortlessly into a moderate panic attack. In less than 10 seconds I went from normal, to feeling uncomfortable, to an overwhelming need to get out.

It rolled right over me. Initially it was similar to claustrophobia, like the times my brothers put a pillow over my head or stuffed me in a footlocker, but quickly became desperate, incapacitating fear. I couldn't control myself. I panicked.

In a relatively short amount of time it wasn't only crowds and dark rooms that got to me. Driving along the Mokulele Highway one afternoon I glanced in the rearview mirror and saw Tiger's empty car seat.

Without pausing to think, I whipped my head around. He wasn't there! Where had I left him? Was it the grocery store? Thoughts raced out of control, and I was instantly in the middle of a panic attack.

When I realized he was in school I settled down right away, but the attacks were branching out and gaining strength. Within a few months I was getting panic attacks so powerful, I thought I was going to die… literally. It felt as if I was suffocating, my worst phobia.

I knew where the phobia came from, and why I had a deathly fear of suffocation. The moment I regained consciousness in the Army evacuation hospital in Long Binh, I saw the large black tube coming out of my nose. It went to a clear plastic box beside the head of my bed. Little colored pistons were going up and down inside. Slowly, I realized the machine was helping me breathe.

The beginning of my phobia was when I got out of sync with the breathing machine. There was no chance of being overpowered by it, of suffocating, but in my befuddled mind that's exactly what seemed to be happening. We were fighting, and I was losing. I didn't know what to do, but as my anxiety rose, so did the effect of the drugs in my blood. I could feel myself relax, and the machine set the pace again.

The next moment I was right back at it. Fortunately a nurse noticed my dilemma, came over, disconnected the tube at my nose, and I began breathing on my own. That's where my suffocation phobia came from, but it had help along the way.

To support the loose sections of my broken jaw, the doctors shaped a small bar of soft metal and placed it behind my teeth, then ran wires between the teeth and around the bar. They left a hole for me to eat where one of my lower teeth, probably tooth 25, had been. It was just large enough to accommodate a straw. With my teeth wired tightly together, plus the bar and all the wire, airflow through my mouth was restricted to the point that, without the assistance of my nose, I couldn't get enough air to breathe comfortably.

When my nose plugged up, I became understandably anxious but never lost it. I knew that if I panicked I'd need more air, the one thing I couldn't get, which would make my panic worse, which would make me want more air. It was a syndrome I wanted to avoid because I believed, with so little air available to begin with, if I put too much demand on the system, I might actually die.

Within a few weeks it wasn't only things like misplacing my son that brought on attacks and suffocation issues. Getting caught in a cloud of dust blowing across the road could do it, just that small amount of air contamination. After my first dozen panic attacks, which grew steadily worse, I decided to see if the Veterans Administration had anything that might help. I described what was happening and talked over different medications with their psychiatrist.

We went through the long list of drugs the VA had already tried on me. None of them had been effective, so he recommended lorazepam, a drug that often worked when others didn't. It was strong and fast acting, which I liked. That way, I could fight the attack on my own for as long as it was practical, then knock it down quickly with lorazepam if it got out of control.

Lorazepam was my drug of choice until I had a panic attack in the middle of my morning exercise routine. The way the attack came on I thought it was going to be bad; however, after the initial rush it leveled off, just hung there. So I kept stretching and breathing; a long slow inhale through my nose, then slowly back out my mouth, in through the nose... and the panic began to fade.

It seemed that the attack was subdued by my deep breathing exercise, something I'd adopted from yoga. To test my theory I successfully used several of my best triggers. When the attacks began to take shape I switched the way I inhaled and exhaled, and the symptoms dropped radically.

From then on, whenever I had an attack that was getting out of control, I began breathing deep and slow. If that didn't work within a few minutes I took a lorazepam or two.

I also worked with a psychologist at the VA clinic on Maui who introduced me to a muscle relaxing technique that reduced tension throughout my body. It wasn't anything major, just one more useful tool.

With those means I could control my panic attacks, but that didn't slow them down. As they grew worse it wasn't unusual for me to fly out of bed from a deep sleep and run out of the room. Often I'd be in the living room or out on the porch before I knew what I was doing.

I couldn't help but wonder what would happen if I ever chose the door to the bedroom porch with its eight foot drop to the ground. Would I wake up before I went over the railing? Not knowing for sure, my rule was, don't sleep on boats and trains, or any place higher than the second floor.

Panic attacks were definitely my biggest problem. I still got angry but didn't fly into rages as often. Intrusive thoughts weren't as threatening and suicidal depressions were things of the past.

My back had also been good; however, I wasn't asking much of it and Maui was warm. It really had no right to complain. Once in a while I picked up something too heavy, or twisted wrong, and the muscles would spasm for a few days. Overall it was hardly a concern, but I still did my daily exercises and saw a chiropractor once or twice a month. I even tried acupuncture, which worked like nothing before or since.

The small, strategically placed needles blocked the pain in my neck, back and legs instantly. They brought so much relief I seemed to rise off the table in a mild state of euphoria. In that sublime moment I felt myself slip beneath the turbulent surface of my life.

As I drifted without sensation in the comfortable depths, I saw a shape in the distance. It was a man, also adrift. There were no distinguishing features but he appeared to be relaxed. It seemed as if an aura of contentment surrounded the figure.

Before long I realized the other entity was none other than me when I was a younger man, before I went to war, and intrinsically we weren't that different. Unfortunately, the VA wouldn't authorize payment for acupuncture, and it was just too expensive otherwise.

With Tiger in preschool I found time to get back to Easy Target. I'd finished it a year earlier, but hadn't sent it out. There were the usual reasons: it needs one more rewrite, I don't know what to do next. However, what really kept me from sending it out was, the book was my sanctuary. A place I could go and let my mind wander freely, far from its preoccupations. That would be gone if I sent it out. It would be over.

There was also the arena of public opinion. Did I really want to find out I was the only one who liked it? But, as luck would have it, the first Maui Writer's Conference was held in a hotel just down the street from where we lived.

I went to the conference hoping to meet an agent or

publisher, but never got to talk to either. However, the attitude of the aspiring authors was contagious. As Kathy put it when she stopped by, "This place reeks of ego."

Whatever it was, I was motivated enough to spend the next few weeks putting together the best query letter I could, then mailed it with a copy of my manuscript to Presidio Press, the self-proclaimed foremost publisher of American military history.

Less than a month later I got a phone call. "Good afternoon," an older man said. "This is Bob Cane. Is this Tom Smith?"

"Yes, it is," I said curtly. I didn't recognize the name or voice and was on my way out the door. "But I was just about to . . ."

"I understand," he interjected. "I'll be brief. We would like to publish your book."

As his words sank in I found myself in a large, ornate theater, standing alone in the center of the stage, right out front, as the entire audience rose to their feet and cheered, "Bravo!" I'm not kidding; that's exactly what went through my mind. It was pretty amazing.

"Tom?" Hearing my name brought me back. I knew I had to say something.

"My mother would be very proud of me," I told my new friend.

Writing Easy Target was a rewarding experience; however, getting published made me feel better about myself than any single accomplishment I could remember… except for my part in raising Tiger and flying helicopters, of course. I should have taken Kathy's advice the first time she suggested I write.

Around then we moved back to Ulupalakua Ranch. My friend Mitch had died and Pardee let us move into the old sugar mill. Within the year our second son was born. Tiger had masterfully capitalized on the guilt of a hard-working woman and talked his hesitant mother into giving it a try. Because of his role in what transpired, Tiger claimed naming rights.

Cougar, every bit as beautiful as his brother, was different from the beginning. Immediately after birth, during the Apgar test, the obstetrician pulled Cougar up by the arms, partially lifting the baby's torso off the examining table to make sure things stayed together. When the doctor relaxed, to his surprise Cougar kept moving towards him, using his own strength to get closer. "Never seen that before," the doctor commented, obviously impressed.

Less than a year later another doctor was checking Cougar's tonsils. As he withdrew the wooden tongue depressor the baby clenched his little gums, broke off the tip, and swallowed it.

Kathy didn't go back to work right away. She used her maternity leave and then, because she had concerns about Cougar's health, took two months of accumulated vacation time.

His problem appeared to be air pollution, which at first was hard to believe on an island in the middle of the Pacific Ocean. However, the sugar plantations were harvesting cane, which entailed burning the standing stalks. The smoke from the green vegetation was thick and frequently blanketed our area. Often there was so much ash in the air it looked like dark snow.

The heaviest burning began not long after Cougar was born and went on for six months. At the same time it was very dry and dusty on the ranch. The air was also full of particulates from the volcanic eruptions on the Big Island. That combination got to the little guy's developing respiratory system. Our normally animated and energetic infant became increasingly weak and listless.

When Kathy's vacation time was over and Cougar's health hadn't changed, she restructured her job to have more time at home. However, before she began work as the refuge's outreach specialist, his condition took a turn for the worse and we had him on a plane to see a specialist in California the next day. His asthma improved, so rather than return to Hawaii and risk his getting sick again we decided to move.

For once we weren't leaving to gratify my need for change. Nevertheless, when we'd decided it was the right thing to do, I looked forward to moving with as much enthusiasm as ever.

After considering Alaska and the coasts of Washington and Oregon, we decided to go back East. I knew my small hometown had a good school, and with the money we saved from Kathy's job, the sale of our condo and the Homer house, along with investments I'd capitalized on in a bull market, we had enough to build a house.

The move seems to have been the right thing to do. Our home is comfortable. We have a few good friends and lots of privacy. Tiger has adjusted to his new environment and friends well. He was class president from middle school to his senior year, captain of the varsity soccer team, a Regents Scholar, and an accomplished recreational skier.

Cougar is also glad we moved. Like his brother, he loves soccer and is very good at the game, plays the ball, is more interested in teamwork than personal glory, and doesn't give up, much less ever slow down. He is also an excellent student, takes pride in doing well, and he's attractive. When Cougar was in kindergarten the teacher had to impose a "no kissing Cougar during class" rule.

Kathy has been using her time well, dividing it between being a mother, some consulting work, public service and pursuing a Doctorate in Environmental Studies. She also runs marathons.

A few months ago during hunting season someone took a shot too close to our house. I got my shotgun and went looking for him. I was as upset as I had been twenty years earlier, yelled and cursed, but didn't shoot up the woods. This time I wasn't out of control. I just wanted to make sure the hunter knew he wasn't welcome in the woods around my home, and took my gun for security.

There are other things. I can't control my startle reflex, I still have a few uninspired intrusive thoughts, loose my temper more than I'd like, even get mild panic attacks now and then, but none of those things control me, or bother me more than they should. I've lived with them for so long, the things inside my head are part of me.

IN HINDSIGHT

Awareness and perception, recognizing the disorder and relating it to myself, helped me face my PTSD. But the process could have been easier.

In Chapter Four I wrote about something that happened at a friend's house not too long after I got back from Vietnam. Across the room from me was a pistol on an end table by the couch. While I looked at the gun something very strange came to mind. I had an urge, actually felt compelled, to pick it up and pull the trigger, repeatedly. Surrealistically I saw the bullets going everywhere, dangerously close to the people around me, and I didn't feel a thing, didn't seem to care. Shocked, and a little scared, I quickly went on to something else.

As chance would have it, that was the right thing to do. What I visualized was similar to the dreams I had in combat, bullets and chaos, obvious extensions of what was going on around me every day. So I dismissed the incident figuring it was an oddity associated with my recent life in a war zone.

At that point in time I saw cause and effect quite well. I didn't know anything about PTSD, and certainly did not think I had a psychological disorder related to combat, but it was easy for me to connect what I'd been doing in Vietnam with the abnormal thought that evening at my friend's. Unfortunately, when the next intrusive image came along and I saw myself stab Kathy in the back, it was fifteen years later and the connection between violent thoughts and the realities of war wasn't there anymore. So I treated the intrusive thought as if it were something entirely new, an atrocious usurper of my mind that had to be dealt with immediately, decisively.

That was a big mistake. Not being able to see the

connection any longer was understandable, and I was right to be concerned. But letting bizarre images and thoughts, basically figments of my imagination, provoke such strong reactions was counter productive. It put me on the defensive and I was no longer in control.

In hindsight, if I'd known about PTSD I would have treated the second round of intrusive thoughts like the first, gone on to something else, not given them credibility. That's how I deal with them now and they never get past the odd thought stage.

Being aware of PTSD's symptoms would have had an effect on my anger too. Knowing that it was part of a disorder would have made it less personal, easier to explain to myself and other people. I doubt that I would have felt under attack, the most prevalent trigger for my anger, as often as I did. And being able to relate my temper to PTSD would have made it easier to apologize constantly, a necessity if you are dealing with the disorder. With a little enlightened counseling I wouldn't have tried so hard to overpower the rage. I would have treated it as I do now, keep it at a distance. When provoked I concentrate on relaxing to the exclusion of everything else, using yoga breathing and other techniques to tone it down because, as soon as I get control, even the least amount, my anger begins to fade.

If I'd known about PTSD from the beginning its symptoms would have been out in the open and not buried within me. This is where perception comes in. Seeing yourself in relation to the disorder is as important as awareness, seeing the disorder itself. Before I knew it was related to PTSD I thought my anger was warranted, that people brought it on themselves. But once I knew that it was a part of the disorder I began to see the anger as my problem, and that it was something I was going to have to deal with.

If you do not recognize this in yourself, PTSD will ruin your life. But if you see the disorder as an entity that you can work with, you will be able to take control one day at a time. Before long it will be yours, not the other way around.

Something else that needs to be addressed is stress, which is usually treated as a secondary issue that goes away once the problem is solved. In situations like PTSD, where the symptoms are so strong and can last indefinitely, stress takes on a life of its own and adds tremendous pressure to everyday events, especially tense situations.

The most effective way I've found to deal with stress is slow deep breathing for immediate relief, and meditation for the long term. I'm not very comfortable in the lotus position and don't like to chant mantras, but I've found enough practical information in Matthieu Ricard's "Why Meditate" to make it work. He was dubbed the happiest man in the world by the media after scoring substantially higher than others in a study involving meditation and brain activity.

What appeals to me is the way Matthieu develops his concept for living in the present, no recriminations from the past or fear of the future, a practice that leaves my mind relatively calm and attentive.

I believe that knowing about PTSD and its symptoms earlier would have helped with my intrusive thoughts, anger and stress problems; however, by the time I began having suicidal depressions and panic attacks I knew quite a bit about the disorder and its influence on my life. Unfortunately that knowledge didn't seem to have much of an impact. I'd tell myself the depressions were part of the disorder, nothing to be concerned about, but I still slipped into the hole. While I was there, logic and reason were never an option. It was the same with panic attacks. But when they were over, knowing about the disorder, that it was something I could survive, was extremely helpful.

Awareness and perception are necessary tools for anyone dealing with PTSD. They are also every bit as important to family and friends. Kept in the dark, wives, husbands and children are in a terrible place. Bound by love, sympathy and a sense of duty, they have little choice but to endure the constant outbursts of anger in silence or leave. Knowing about the disorder helps them understand what is going on and why. It allows them to develop strategies of their own for dealing with the issues, which gives the people who care about you a chance to help.

Recognizing PTSD and relating to it has been a long and difficult process; however, through distractions I began mitigating some of the effects of the disorder long before I was aware of its symptoms. Realizing their relevance took more time because most of the distractions came to me naturally.

When I walked out of Walter Reed Army Hospital and bought my Porsche, the way I drove changed. The car held the road as if it were on rails. It begged to go through corners at twice the speed I was used to, and the sound of six downdraft carburetors wide open was mesmerizing. I told myself I drove fast because the car could handle it, because it felt good. But I also drove fast because it required all of my attention.

I drove much farther too. At first I was in the car for long periods of time to get away from the depressing atmosphere of the hospital. Both my roommates at Walter Reed were nice young men who'd been shot in the head and lost their sight. It was spring outside, cherry blossoms were blooming, the sky was bright blue, and they couldn't see it, never would. That was too much for me.

Before long the extended drives became a haven. As I drove the back roads of Virginia my mind roamed where it chose, randomly responding to the endless amount of visual stimulation gliding by. Memories came and went, plans were formed, and sometimes I just drove. While the back roads were an endless source of distractions, I found that the freeways were better for daydreaming.

After I got out of the Army my road trips became longer. There wasn't anything wrong with my home in the mountains, but after a few months in the same place I felt restless, irritable, and went on road trips, often across the country, to leave those feelings behind. When that wasn't enough, I began moving. Every time I changed environments, New York to Colorado, to California, back to New York, to Borneo, back to California, to Alaska, back to New York, life seemed to improve.

Before I met Kathy I changed locations on an average of twice a year. After we got together we didn't move as often and I seldom went on long road trips by myself. That's when I learned to appreciate less extreme forms of distraction, like domestic chores and projects around the house. Things that kept my hands and mind busy, made the day mine.

Another distraction that came to me effortlessly was drinking. If I didn't have anything else to do I always appreciated a cold beer. Later in the day I usually switched to whiskey because I liked the way the potent fluid spread quickly through my body, mixing with the tension, absorbing it. How it left behind a less-encumbered self at the end of the day.

In my defense, I was raised in a culture that embraced the consumption of alcohol. There was always a lot of it around and getting drunk was an adventure with few repercussions as long as nobody got hurt. After Vietnam the bars were my social life until I began to drink too much. When it became excessive, instead of relieving tension and being a catalyst for social interaction, the alcohol became an accelerant for my deteriorating attitude and an open door for my anger. The worse things got the more I drank, until that hung-over morning in Alaska with my shotgun, when I felt like picking it up and shooting myself. That's when I quit drinking for a year, telling myself that if I ever got that drunk again I would quit forever.

The change was easier than I thought. Within days I barely missed having a drink and felt better for it; however, there was a noticeable void, especially during the long, slow hours after the sun went down. So I began smoking pot again.

I ran into marijuana when I was a teenager, smoked a little in college, and a fair amount of it in Vietnam where it often took the place of alcohol, which was rationed. After the war I went back to whiskey and beer; however, when I had to quit drinking I began smoking the nefarious weed once more.

At first it was a simple swap of distractions, alcohol for cannabis. Before long though, I found that smoking a little pot, not getting completely stoned, complemented many of the things I did on a daily basis. It allowed me to focus on mundane chores and complex projects alike for long periods of time without losing interest. I could literally put everything else out of mind and distance myself from unnecessary thoughts and emotions. To a point, pot even seemed to help me manage my anger.

It's important to keep in mind that everyone is different. Where seclusion, low levels of stress, and family have helped me live with the symptoms of Post Traumatic Stress Disorder, someone else might benefit more from life in a city, a demanding job and bachelorhood.

Also worth noting is the difference between distraction and escape. Long drives, exercise, most tasks and chores, along with moderate use of stimulants, are distractions. Excessive drinking and over use of drugs are escapes. They both mask the disorder's symptoms, keep them out of mind, but distractions are passive and sustainable whereas escapes are not.

- 33 -

Without awareness and perception I wouldn't have been able to see PTSD or how it related to me. If not for distractions the disorder's symptoms would have overwhelmed me. But only relationships could keep me company, provide friendship, comfort and make life interesting in ways nothing else can.

I was incredibly lucky to run into Zach before leaving the army. I had no idea how important his companionship would be to me, the security he'd provided or the loneliness he would keep at bay. Only in hindsight can I truly appreciate the love and affection my dog gave without reservation. Zach was the best of friends and I will always miss him.

My relationship with Darcie cost me quite a bit in terms of pride and money, but I learned a few things and, all in all, came out ahead because she set me up to appreciate someone like Kathy.

I might have been lost without Zach, and I certainly learned a lot about people, myself included, with Darcie, but it was Kathy who helped me through the roughest part of my life. Left alone in the grip of PTSD my thoughts would have consumed me. Most likely I'd have died early of something related to alcohol. Although a number of people could have helped me avoid that fate, Kathy did more than keep me company during a difficult time. She gave me something to look forward to. My wife had her own life, was independent and excelled at what she did. I believed that, when I got control of the disorder, my life would be more like hers.

Kathy was also a mirror of sorts. The confusion in her eyes when my mood suddenly shifted, the surprise at the sudden outbursts of anger, and apprehension when I was in a fit of rage... in her reactions I could see a clear picture of the person she was dealing with. At first I took what I saw as criticism, believing that her natural reactions were unwarranted, hypercritical. Eventually I came to see them as indicators of just how far I was from normal.

My relationship with our children was similar. I gained from interacting with them, while they got to practice patience and learn what it's like to live with an emotionally unstable person.

I have been fortunate in my relationships with my family. Regrettably, that's not the norm for veterans dealing with PTSD. Anger, that sense of being wronged and under attack, is so pervasive and long lived that it defines, and invariably destroys, most relationships. But it doesn't have to be that way. We can change.

The medical branch of the Veterans Administration is another important relationship. The most consistent source of help, other than my family, has been the VA's doctors, nurses, and technicians. Their resources are good, mission clear, and the help is free. Like any large underfunded organization there are problems. Some hospitals and staff are better than others, but they are all there to help and, more often than not, doing their best. Even Dr. Vandervort, the director of the hospital in Hawaii and frequent recipient of my wrath, was a decent guy. Like many in the VA health care system he was dealing with numerous diverse and evolving issues while bound by strict constraints. As busy as he was, I should have been more appreciative of his time.

The other part of the Veterans Administration I dealt with extensively, Claims and Adjudication, has been both friend and foe, but mostly foe. Working with them requires two things: patience and proficiency in the use of the Code of Federal Regulations.

When I addressed an issue using my own words the people in Claims didn't seem to get the point, misinterpreted what I'd written, and invariably reacted inanely. However, when I used the CFR that dealt with the same issue, and demonstrated how my problem was related, their response was often prompt and usually succinct.

Claims and Adjudication use the Code of Federal Regulations in all their decisions. They don't have any other standard. They literally can't make a decision unless it fits the CFRs. There is little you can do about the endless amount of time it takes for claims to be processed, but using the government's regulations can reduce the amount of wasted effort.

In hindsight I have reduced my years of experience with PTSD into several tenets: awareness, perception, distractions, and relationships. I did this for insight, not to minimize the scope or impact of the disorder. Similarly, I have tried to put its development into perspective.

A lot of things happened to me in Vietnam. I experienced new heights in confidence and accomplished some amazing feats. I also had the shit scared out of me quite often and was seriously injured. However, when I wrote "Easy Target" I noticed something else, an element of fear growing steadily throughout my tour of duty.

The source of the fear wasn't just getting shot up and crashing a few times. Those were terrifying moments and the danger very real; however, I was relatively prepared for that. Combat is a game of sorts and I had a lot of say in how it was played. I decided when and where to fight, and when to break it off.

The fear I saw in myself was deeper, more consistent than those threats. It was something I had no control over, the world I lived in. I woke up to the smells and sounds of a forward base in a combat zone. I never got used to my first impression of the day... that I shouldn't be there. Before I put my feet on the floor I looked for things that might harm me. Every time I climbed into my helicopter I knew that death was out there waiting. I lived in an environment of fear. There were no breaks; with rockets, mortars and sapper attacks, not even in sleep.

In the beginning the fear was primarily apprehension, a cautious approach to things; however, over time it grew out of control. I became superstitious, followed rituals religiously and carried things I associated with close calls and good luck. Later it became paranoia, feelings of dread and imminent demise for no apparent reason.

At the time I didn't know that fear was part of my fight or flight response, a survival instinct intrinsic to human nature, and that there are both fear and anger in this natural reaction to a threat. Anger being the main component of the fight response, and fear the flight part of it. Although the fight or flight response is natural it isn't normal and, as a psychiatrist recently told me, "The problem is the chemicals released in our brain to help keep us alive under threatening conditions, when used too frequently, can damage parts of the brain involved in managing emotion and thinking. There are studies out there that conclude prolonged exposure can result in permanent change. As I understand it, the result is a perpetual state of fight or flight."

For a year I lived on a steady diet of fear and anger. Considering my experiences it's not hard to imagine that the chemistry of my brain has been altered, or that my fight or flight response is permanent. A transformation of my cerebral functions also helps explain everything from my instant reaction to a loud or startling noise to my inability to see PTSD clearly, and why, to this day, it's nearly impossible for me to control my extreme reactions to any threat, real or perceived.

Until there was the connection between Post Traumatic Stress Disorder and brain function, I believed the disorder was a product of conditioning. That the symptoms I experienced were part of a conflict between my life as a civilian, soldier, then civilian again. It seemed to me that the anger and fear I experienced in combat came back with me because they were woven into the fabric of my life, that I could no more leave them behind than I could the skills I'd acquired as a pilot. But that belief does little to clarify why I have been unable to change my behavior, to essentially recondition myself to a civilian's mentality, whereas a permanent change in the way my brain functions explains the difficulty in changing my mentality.

Now that I have a better understanding of what the problem is, I no longer see the symptoms of PTSD as a shortcoming on my part, or a failure of any kind. It is the price I pay for excessive use of my fight or flight response, and there is no apparent way of undoing that. I am a different person and can live with it. There are even some positive aspects to the disorder. My mind has been getting plenty of exercise, life certainly hasn't been boring, and I've often put my frenetic energy to good use doing everything from chores around the house to writing books.

I also got to spend a lot of time with my sons while they were growing up, a unique and fulfilling experience for me. However, over the years I couldn't help but wonder how Tiger, who saw so much of my anger, felt about our time together. So, before he left for college I asked him how much my involvement with PTSD had adversely impacted his life.

After assuring me it wasn't a lot, he said. "If anything it's made me a better person."

"How?" I asked, surprised.

"I'm pretty sure I'm tougher than I would've been," he replied. "That comes in handy. And I relate to stressed people pretty well." He laughed.

"Yes, you do," I agreed. "And thank you for that."

My feelings about his response were mixed. I was relieved to hear that my son was happy with himself, and me, but I'd been hoping he'd forgotten about the anger, that I had changed enough over the years.

"Well, at least my temper's better now," I added, fishing for a compliment. His response was a broad grin. "Damn it, Tiger," I exclaimed. "You know it is!"

He laughed again, and gave me a hug, "Sure, Dad. Whatever you say."

The End

Made in the USA
Columbia, SC
03 August 2022

64344287R00098